HUMBERSIDE LIBRARIES

Prescription for Poor Health:
The Crisis for Homeless
Families

- 3 FEB 1990
11 JUN 1991
20 MAY 1993
13 MAY 1994
18 OCT 1994
20 1
16 FEB
-8 M
-9 DEC 1994
3 DEC 1994
22 MAR
-6 JAN 1994
24 JAN
-8 APR 1993
28 JAN 1994
19 APR 1993
5 MAR 1995
10 MAY 1995
20 AUG 1995

B26551124

ALS No.   B26551124

This item should be returned on or before the last date stamped above. If not in demand it may be renewed for a further period by personal application, by telephone, or in writing. The author, title, above number and date due back should be quoted.   LS/3

PRESCRIPTION FOR POOR HEALTH

PRESCRIPTION FOR POOR HEALTH

THE CRISIS FOR HOMELESS FAMILIES

EDITOR: JEAN CONWAY

LONDON FOOD COMMISSION ◆ MATERNITY ALLIANCE ◆ SHAC ◆ SHELTER

Prescription for poor health
The health crisis for homeless families

Editor: Jean Conway

This report was written by Isobel Cole-Hamilton of the **London Food Commission**, Lyn Durward of the **Maternity Alliance**, Jean Conway of **SHAC**, and Jonathan Stearn of **Shelter**.

Published jointly by London Food Commission, the Maternity Alliance, SHAC and Shelter in June 1988.

© LFC, Maternity Alliance, SHAC & Shelter

Typesetting, artwork and printing: RAP Ltd., Rochdale

Cover design by Peter Brawne

Trade distribution: Turnaround 01-609 7836

ISBN 0 948857 18 8

Organisations

♦ **THE LONDON FOOD COMMISSION** is a voluntary organisation, set up in early 1985 to be an independent source of research, information, education and advice on food. It is governed by a council and management committee elected by member organisations to represent London's community and voluntary groups, food sector trade unions, statutory bodies and interested individuals and professionals.

♦ **THE MATERNITY ALLIANCE** is an independent national organisation which campaigns for improvement in rights and services for mothers, fathers, and babies. It works for better provision before conception, and during pregnancy, childbirth and the first year of life. Over 70 national organisations have come together in the Alliance to promote the interests of parents and babies; to campaign for policies designed to meet their needs and to provide a forum for discussion between the users and providers of services.

♦ **SHAC (THE LONDON HOUSING AID CENTRE)** was established in 1969 as London's first housing advice centre to provide a broad range of help and advice on housing matters. Since then more than 115,000 people with housing problems have been helped. SHAC also undertakes research into the major housing issues of the day and provides information and training for a wide range of voluntary and statutory organisations.

♦ **SHELTER** is the largest of the national housing campaigning organisations. It has called for an end to the use of bed and breakfast for homeless families.

Acknowledgements

Much of this report is based on interviews with homeless women and with health professionals; we are grateful that they gave their time to talk to us. Contacts with the women in hotels were made through the following:

London Borough of Brent, Housing Department; London Borough of Haringey, Housing Department; Manchester City Council, Homeless Families Section; Health visitors at the Queensway Health Centre, Southend; Bayswater Project, Playgroup; Clapham Community Project; Field Lane Centre, Kings Cross; Shelter, S.E.; Shelter, N.W.; Ealing Housing Advisory Service; Tower Hamlets Homeless Families Campaign; Rama Sharma.

Additional interviewing was done by Paula Uddin, Karen Smith, Nadine Nylander and Laura Mason. Madeline Drake gave valuable advice on the interview questionnaire.

We also thank Ellis Friedman and Joan Armstrong in South Manchester, and Luise Parsons in the City and Hackney Health Authority for their help with the analysis of health records, and all the health visitors and record clerks in London and Manchester who helped us trace the health records. Our thanks are also due to David Wells from Southwark, John Grigg from the British Dietetic Association and Tim Lang from the London Food Commission who gave valuable comments on the dietary analysis; also to Roma Iskander of the Health Visitors Association and Peter Elton from Manchester who commented on the records analysis.

Many thanks to those who helped with typing, especially Melanie Hare and Nadine Nylander who brought the whole report together. Jean Shapiro's help with the editing was invaluable. Victoria Ramsay was a brilliant sub-editor.

We are grateful to the King Edward's Hospital Fund for London for a grant towards the cost of producing the report and to the Calouste Gulbenkian foundation for supporting the research.

Contents

List of tables   xi

Recommendations   xv

Chapter 1
Introduction and background to the study   1

The housing crisis   1
Poor housing, poor health   2
Poverty, diet and health   4
Special projects to help people living in hotels   5
This study   6
Interviews with women living in hotels   7
    The sample
    The interviews
Interviews with professionals   10
    Midwives and health visitors
    General practitioners
    Environmental health officers
Examination of health records   11
    Using health records
    The areas included
    The analysis of health records
    The mothers and children

Chapter 2
Conditions in bed and breakfast hotels   21

Introduction and summary   21

Amenities 23
Heating and hygiene 24
Food 25
   Storing food
   Preparing food
   Cooking and kitchens
Safety and security 29
   Physical safety
   Fire risks
   Security
Overcrowding in hotel rooms 30
How long families stay in hotels 33
Employment 35
Money 36
Local authority action on standards 39

Chapter 3
The health of homeless women in hotels 41

Introduction and summary 41
Physical health 42
Mental health 44
Personal relationships 46

Chapter 4
Hotel life for pregnant women 49

Introduction and summary 49
The women's own experiences 50
Pregnant women and diet 52
The views of health professionals 52
Information collected from health records 54

Chapter 5
Food and diet — 57

Introduction and summary — 57
The women's diets — 60
Factors affecting the women's diets — 62
    Facilities for preparing and cooking food
    Money
    Age
    Ethnic origin
    Meal patterns
The women's feelings about their diets — 70
Comments from health professionals — 72

Chapter 6
Children's health and diet — 75

Introduction and summary — 75
Newborn babies in hotels — 76
    Birthweight
    Mothers' and health professionals' concerns about newborn babies
Babies' and children's illnesses — 79
The children's behaviour and development — 81
Accidents — 83
Play facilities for children — 83
The children's food and diet — 84
Health records of the children's development — 85
Immunisation and vaccination — 86

Chapter 7
Health care — 89

Introduction and summary — 89
The women's perceptions of available health care — 90
Problems with primary health care: GPs — 92
    Registering with a GP

Organising GP services
Problems with primary health care: health visitors and
   midwives   96
   Caseloads
   Lack of information
Local initiatives to improve health care   99

Chapter 8
Environmental health action on hotel standards   105

Introduction and summary   105
Environmental health practices in the study areas   107
   Westminster
   Camden
   Manchester
   Southend
Limitations on local authority action   112
The need for Government action   113

Summary   117

Appendix 1: Questionnaire for women living in hotels   **125**
Appendix 2: Data collection sheet for health records   **133**

List of tables

Chapter 1
1.1　　Household types in the interview survey
1.2　　Ethnic origin of women in the survey
1.3　　Ethnic origin and household type in the survey
1.4　　Percentage of Indian, Bangladeshi and Pakistani children included in the records analysis.

Chapter 2
2.1　　Access to amenities in the survey
2.2　　Food storage space used by the women in the survey
2.3　　Problems experienced in storing food in the survey
2.4　　Kitchen facilities available to the women in the survey
2.5　　Overcrowding in the survey
2.6　　Time spent in hotels so far, in the survey
2.7　　Income and type of household in the survey

Chapter 3
3.1　　Women's symptoms of stress

Chapter 4
4.1　　Number of women with problems recorded in pregnancy and labour (Manchester sample only).

Chapter 5
5.1　　Consumption of fruit and vegetables compared with intakes in the north of England in 1984.
5.2　　Actual consumption of food the day before the interview.

5.3 Relationship between the quality of the women's diets and their use of kitchen facilities.
5.4 Relationship between types of food and the number of meals the women cooked each week.
5.5 Relationship between the quality of the women's diets and the ages of the women.
5.6 Meal patterns related to ethnic origin
5.7 The relationship between meal patterns and overall quality of the women's diets.
5.8 The women's feelings about their diet
5.9 Problems connected with food and eating experienced by women with good, poor and average diets.

Chapter 6
6.1 Birthweight in the records analysis
6.2 Children with no health assessment
6.3 Children with no immunisations or vaccinations

Foreword

HOMELESSNESS HAS doubled in England in the last decade; a quarter of a million people are recognised by local authorities as being homeless; probably the figure is much higher than this for many, such as childless couples, are not included in these data. A proportion of these homeless families are being housed in poor accommodation, in bed and breakfast hotels which cater specifically for those with nowhere else to live. In such hotels, facilities are basic; space for young children, cooking and washing facilities are deficient while there is a lack of privacy. Water for washing is hard to get and cleanliness is difficult. This was a big city phenomenon but has now spread like other urban blights.

This report details experiences of couples or single mothers and their families living in such accommodation. Interviews were made with those living in bed and breakfast and with the health professionals who care for them. Health records were assessed to give indices of health and development which were compared with similar children in the general population. Hence, details of diet and appalling accommodation could be analysed. The special problems of women who became pregnant under these environmental conditions are highlighted.

This report on bed and breakfast accommodation is to help local authorities and central government. It should be read by all who care about people in the 1980s. In our society many are being brushed under the carpet during the general boom in prosperity of the middle and upper classes. We have never been a uniform society; whilst the upper classes control the media, we must make an extra effort to find more information about the lives of all members of society otherwise the structure will deteriorate. Remember what happened to the Black Report; we must do better this time.

Geoffrey Chamberlain, MD, FRCS, FRCOG,
Professor of Obstetrics & Gynaecology,
St. George's Hospital Medical School,
London.

Recommendations

Local authorities
Local authorities should step up their efforts to use every means available to provide homeless families with suitable permanent housing. If temporary accommodation has to be used, alternatives to bed and breakfast should be found wherever possible, especially for pregnant women and young babies. Schemes could include short-life housing and joint schemes with housing associations and the private sector. The following recommendations relate to authorities which have no alternative to the use of bed and breakfast hotels as a last resort for the homeless.

Main recommendations
♦ Where families with young children have to be placed in bed and breakfast hotels, they should be given well-equipped rooms with storage space, a table and chairs. Where the room is above the second floor there should be a working lift.

♦ Council resources should be directed to meet the needs of homeless families in hotels, such as:

+ providing extra social workers in the areas where hotels accommodate the homeless

+ developing community centres with cooking facilities and play areas
+ increasing nursery provision
+ supporting initiatives by the voluntary sector aimed at helping homeless hotel families
+ directing food and health policies to the needs of the hotel homeless
+ co-ordinating services.

◆ Minimum environmental health standards for bed and breakfast hotels should be drawn up and enforced and hotels inspected at least every six months. Hotels inside or outside the borough which do not meet these standards should not be used. These include:

+ compliance with fire regulations
+ safety standards for equipment in bedrooms, kitchens and bathrooms
+ the prevention of overcrowding
+ restrictions on the number of people sharing facilities
+ the provision of well-equipped kitchens with food storage
+ the provision of safe, well-equipped children's indoor play facilities with trained staff where possible
+ working public telephones within easy reach of all rooms
+ standards of cleanliness and safety
+ management and personnel standards, such as respect for privacy of homeless families.

◆ Local authorities should set up a co-ordinating group which brings together all the agencies dealing with services for homeless families in hotels — housing, education, social services and health authorities, together with voluntary and community groups and homeless people themselves. The group should meet regularly to plan and monitor services and should include representatives of all the relevant workers — health visitors, midwives, GPs, community physicians, community dieticians, environmental health officers, social workers, psychiatric health and social workers, education welfare officers, teachers and housing department staff.

In addition

♦ Good communications should be established between homeless families in hotels and the housing department so that the families are informed about their housing situation, and have some idea of how long they will have to stay in hotels. They should also be given written information about the standards they should expect in the hotel and how they can pursue a complaints procedure where necessary.

♦ Housing departments should notify health authorities, social services, environmental health and education authorities within one week of families moving into, out of and between hotels. Having regard to confidentiality and safety, the information should include all the relevant details of the families.

♦ All those coming into contact with homeless families in hotels, including reception and clerical staff, should be given suitable training to increase their understanding and avoid stereotyping of homeless families and those from ethnic minority communities. Where appropriate interpreters should be easily available to both council staff and the families, and literature translated.

♦ Authorities should set up channels for exchanging information on ways of improving services for homeless families in hotels.

Health authorities

Many mothers and children face problems with access

to health care; the problem for homeless families is simply more acute. Rather than proposing separate development of specialist health services for homeless families, these recommendations seek to improve access and services for all families.

Main recommendations

♦ Health authorities should recognise the particular needs of homeless families in bed and breakfast hotels and direct resources to meet these needs, such as:

+ employing extra staff including health visitors, midwives, linkworkers and support staff to provide high levels of support for homeless families. (It is recommended that there should be at least one health visitor for 50 homeless families or one to a yearly throughput of 200 families)
+ providing areas with a high concentration of homeless families with locally based outreach services, such as antenatal and baby clinics, with extra services such as a creche and English teaching for pregnancy classes where appropriate
+ providing mother and baby centres linked to baby clinics where children can play, meals can be cooked and women can meet
+ developing a food and health policy specifically to address the needs of the hotel homeless as a group at nutritional risk.

♦ Family Practitioner Committees should be encouraged to improve care for homeless families in hotels, including:

+ ensuring easy registration with a local GP
+ minimising the use of temporary registration
+ recognising the additional workload which homeless families may present and providing extra support where necessary

+ providing training and education for GPs to increase their understanding and avoid stereotyping
+ speeding up the time it takes for medical records to be transferred from one GP to another.

♦ District health authorities and Family Practitioner Committees should co-ordinate their services to the hotel homeless and both should actively participate in the co-ordinating groups with local authorities and other agencies as recommended above.

In addition:

♦ Health authorities should be flexible in the organisation of maternity and child care, for example:

+ allow pregnant women to refer themselves to midwives where they do not have a GP, and health visitors to refer such women to hospital antenatal clinics
+ allow women to refer themselves to community dieticians where they do not have a GP
+ allow pregnant women and mothers of children under five who have to live in bed and breakfast hotels to hold their own and their children's health records.

♦ Information about local health services and advice on how to protect and improve their health while living in such accommodation should be provided to families living in hotels, directly, through other agencies and by displaying the information in the hotels.

♦ All those coming into contact with homeless families in hotels should be given suitable training as recommended above for local authorities. Similarly interpreters should be easily available and literature translated where appropriate.

♦ Health authorities should keep up-to-date records of the numbers and ages of homeless people living in hotels in their area and monitor illnesses, accidents, hospital attendances and admissions amongst homeless families as a basis for measuring their health needs and planning appropriate services.

◆ Health authorities should set up channels for exchanging information on ways of improving services for homeless families in hotels.

Central government

Homeless families are living in bed and breakfast hotels simply because of the lack of affordable housing to rent. This report has shown how inadequate housing conditions impair women's and children's health and how the extra costs of living in hotels reduce families' resources for leading a full and healthy life. A clear commitment to tackle the problems of homeless families is urgently needed from Central Government.

Main recommendations

◆ It is a fundamental recommendation of this study that the Government should design legislation and provide the resources to ensure that people have permanent homes to live in. This must include:

+ enabling local authorities to provide housing for those in need
+ giving local authorities nomination rights to other forms of rented accommodation
+ ensuring that councils allocate housing and make nominations according to need and that anyone in the area can register on the council waiting list
+ enabling people on low incomes to buy their homes
+ reversing the recent cuts in Housing Benefits so that the

system meets actual rents and low income people can afford adequate housing in the area they wish to live in.

♦ The Government should introduce new legislation on environmental health standards in houses in multiple occupation including hotels, to include:

+ a duty on councils to register and regularly inspect all houses in multiple occupation
+ higher standards of fire safety
+ improved standards for the provision of amenities, occupancy levels and management
+ streamlining the procedures by which councils can enforce these standards and tenants can initiate action
+ the right to compensation and to rehousing if tenants are made homeless as a result of action to improve conditions.

Local authorities should be provided with the resources to back up these measures.

♦ Health Authority funding by Central Government (through the "Resource Allocation Working Party" system) should recognise the health needs of homeless people living in bed and breakfast hotels and give additional resources to areas with large numbers of such families.

♦ The social security system should reflect the extra expenses of living in bed and breakfast accommodation, perhaps through a new premium within the Income Support system (and through the Housing Benefit system after April 1989) to take account of:

+ the extra cost of a healthy diet where cooking facilities are limited

+ the extra cost of special equipment such as slow cookers and well insulated kettles which can be safely used and easily stored
+ extra travel costs to visit health services, social services, and family or friends in a placing authority
+ extra costs for access to play facilities for children where none are available in the bed and breakfast hotel.

In addition

♦ The Department of Environment should ensure that local authorities follow the Code of Guidance to Part 3 of the 1985 Housing Act which says that bed and breakfast accommodation should only be used for very short periods of time and only in exceptional circumstances.

♦ The DOE and DHSS should encourage the provision of services which help homeless people in hotels, monitor new initiatives and promote examples of good practice, backed up by extra resources where appropriate.

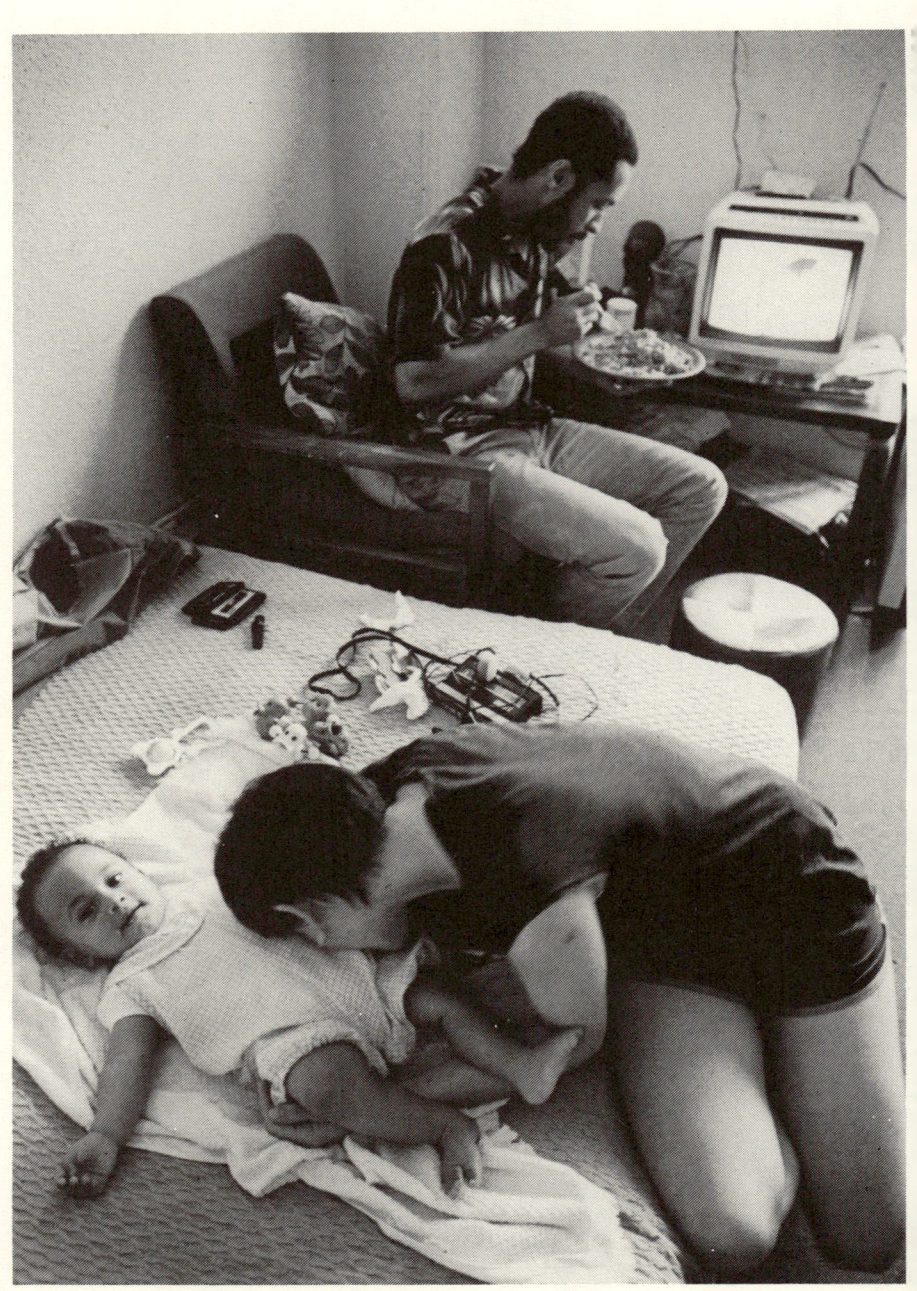

Family living in a bedsit. Earls Court. London 1986.

CHAPTER 1

Introduction and background to the study

"If we are really committed to a healthy society we cannot allow homelessness." (Health visitor)

The housing crisis

HOMELESSNESS IN Great Britain is increasing rapidly. In 1986 over 100,000 households were accepted as homeless by the local authorities in England — nearly twice as many as in 1979.[1] This figure represents perhaps as many as a quarter of a million people. They include the "priority groups" whom local authorities are obliged to accept as homeless (those pregnant, or with children, or vulnerable through age, illness or handicap). However, many childless people are not accepted by local authorities and the true number of homeless people is considerably greater than these figures suggest.

One index of homelessness is the number of people living in some form of board and lodging accommodation, which is generally seen as housing of last resort. The number of supplementary benefit recipients living in board and lodgings in Great Britain increased from 49,000 in 1979 to 127,000 in 1985. Within this figure at least 22,000 are estimated to be living in some form of hotel or guest house. These are not luxury hotels, but a new form of bed and breakfast market often catering specifically for those who have nowhere else to live and who can claim some support from the DHSS to pay the bill. Bed and breakfast residents are mainly concentrated in London and the big cities but more and more people are now living in hotels in all parts of the country.

Hotel residents may have found the accommodation themselves because they could not find anywhere permanent to live, or they may have been placed there by a local authority which has accepted responsibility for rehousing them but has nowhere permanent to offer in the short run. The numbers placed in hotels by local authorities in England has increased sharply to over 10,000 at the end of 1987.[2] The length of time that people stay in hotels has also been increasing and many families are now having to stay for two or more years.

Conditions faced by homeless people in such accommodation are often horrific. Recent government research into hotels and other houses in multiple occupation (HMOs) found that 81 per cent (300,000) lacked proper means of escape from fire; 61 per cent (220,000) had inadequate essential amenities; 59 per cent (197,000) were unfit or in disrepair and four per cent (13,000) were in such a bad condition they should be taken over by councils using control orders.[3]

Poor housing, poor health

Since the middle of the last century there has been concern about the relationship between housing conditions and health. Initially, this focused on the effects of poor water and sanitation, overcrowding and dampness. More recently there has been increasing evidence of the bad effects of living in run-down high-rise flats, such as depression and respiratory disease.[4]

As the numbers living in hotels has increased, so has the concern that this form of accommodation presents particular health risks. There are three main reasons for this:

◆ conditions in hotels are often very poor. Facilities for storing, preparing or cooking food are frequently limited or non-existent; washing facilities are unsatisfactory, and there is extreme overcrowding. General maintenance is poor, resulting in hazards, especially for young children, and fire precautions are often inadequate. Lack of play space and overcrowding also contribute to the high risk of accidents for children;

◆ those who live in hotels tend to be people who cannot afford any better kind of housing, such as the unemployed, those on low wages, large families and those experiencing language or cultural barriers. Even in normal circumstances, such people are vulnerable to health risks;

◆ people who have to live in hotels find it stressful and depressing, making them more prone to poor health.

These factors have been well documented.[5] One recent study of life in a large hotel in West London gave a clear account of the poor physical conditions in the hotel, the problems of people living there, their experiences of racial and sexual harassment, and their uncertainty about their future.[6]

Reports in the past concerned with infant health and mortality frequently noted the relationship between poor health and poor housing. At the beginning of this century one official report stated:

"Excessive infant mortality occurs in tenement and other small dwellings, especially where water is distant to fetch and remove, where cleanliness is consequently difficult,

and where food cannot be satisfactorily stored."
Second report on infant and child mortality, supplement to the 42nd annual report of the Local Government Board 1912-13.

Over 80 years later this might easily be describing some of the bed and breakfast housing surveyed for this report. This new type of accommodation has yet to be recognised as a major influence on health in present-day government reports.

Poverty, diet and health

Along with growing recognition of the links between housing and health, there has been continuing concern about the relationship between poverty and health. This has recently become the subject of increasing debate as unemployment and the number of people living on Supplementary Benefit has risen. Some of these issues were highlighted by the Government's working group on inequalities and health which reported in 1980, and were reassessed by the Health Education Council in 1987.[7] The British Medical Association has recently published a major study of the effects of deprivation on health.[8]

In addition, diet has been identified as a crucial factor.[9] While the British diet in general has been criticised as unhealthy, there are now a number of studies which show that the diet of people on low incomes is improving more slowly than that of the population in general and calls have been made for a national food and health policy.[10] Poverty may also mean that people cannot afford adequate heating or clothing, and there is evidence to show that the poor have less access to good health care than the rest of the population.[11]

Housing acts as a crucial link between poverty and health because, as shown by successive house condition surveys, poor people tend to live in the worst housing.[12] Those who have failed to secure any form of permanent housing — the homeless — are in the worst position of all, and are amongst the poorest and most vulnerable in society.

Special projects to help people living in hotels

There have been some initiatives to help hotel residents cope with their conditions. The Bayswater Project, set up in 1984 in a part of London with a high concentration of homeless families living in hotels, has a small team of people providing housing and welfare advice and runs a playgroup for families with young children. In 1987 Paddington and North Kensington Health Authority set up a Special Health Care Team in the Bayswater area. A similar project has been established in the Earls Court area of West London, and the London Borough of Brent has also set up a centre for homeless families in Bayswater. The Thomas Coram Foundation, founded in 1739 to care for "exposed and deserted young children", has become concerned with the problems of families living in hotels in central London, and commissioned a survey of children in hotels which found their health to be seriously at risk.[13] The various agencies concerned with hotel families in London are now working together and exchanging information.

The London boroughs have jointly considered how the social services should respond to the problem of hotel residents. This includes the need for greater social work support; for collation of information about local facilities such as GPs, hospitals and schools, and for better liaison between the social services department in the borough which has accepted the family as homeless, and in the borough where the family may be living in a hotel. Several London boroughs are also setting up special teams of social workers to work with homeless families, including Camden, which has already established a mobile support scheme.

A number of recent reports have highlighted the inadequacy

of the health care available to single homeless people.[14] In some areas attempts have been made to meet the health needs of these people. One example is the Great Chapel Street Medical Centre in central London, which provides a range of services specifically for the single homeless. A recent examination of primary health care for homeless single people in London stresses the need for a new strategic approach, based on comprehensive locally-based services which cater for the whole community, without segregating the homeless from those with housing.[15]

When homeless families include children, health visitors are often their main contact with the health services and the Health Visitors Association has become increasingly concerned about the health of families living in hotels.[16] Some District Health Authorities have also recognised the particular health needs of hotel residents. Chapter 7 gives details of some of the special services which have been established.

These initiatives, while of value in themselves, do not represent an adequate response to the needs of the increasing number of people who have to live in hotels for long periods of time. There has been no co-ordinated attempt to identify the needs of hotel residents, and to examine the best way of responding to these needs.

This study

The study described in this report examines the needs of homeless hotel residents in relation to health. It focuses on mothers and children under five years old, a group thought to be particularly at risk. The study has three main elements:

◆ an interview survey of women who were pregnant or had children under five who had been living in bed and breakfast hotels for several months. This gathered information about the facilities in the hotel, illnesses and problems experienced by the women and their children, access to health services, and diet. (See Appendix 1;)

♦ interviews with a range of professionals who have contact with women and children living in hotels, including health visitors, GPs, midwives, paediatricians and environmental health officers, in order to identify the issues of major concern to them, and to learn from their experiences;

♦ examination of health records for pregnant women and children. This allows comparison of a number of measures of health and development between those living in hotels and similar people in the general population.

This report, therefore, combines qualitative and quantitative information on the health problems of those living in hotels and evaluates current services. A number of recommendations are made for improving health services for this group.

The study focuses on three areas: London, Manchester and Southend. London has the greatest concentration of families living in hotels; it is estimated that the London boroughs currently have over 6,000 families placed in hotels and the number is rising rapidly. Manchester is included because attempts have been made there to bring together the health and housing services for hotel residents in the city. Southend illustrates another area outside London with a concentration of hotel residents: at the end of 1986, 79 households had been placed in hotels by Southend-on-Sea Council and there are many more living in hotels in the town who have not been placed there by the council because the council has no legal obligation to assist them.

Interviews with women living in hotels

The sample

A total of 57 women living in bed and breakfast hotels

were interviewed: 39 in London, nine in Manchester and nine in Southend. At the time, all had children under five years old or were pregnant, and all had lived in hotels for at least four months. The women were contacted through a wide range of sources including local groups working with homeless people, local authorities and health visitors, and also through direct contact in local centres and baby clinics. In this way the sample includes those who are in touch with support services and those who are more isolated. Whilst the sample is not necessarily statistically representative, an attempt was made to reflect the range of people living in hotels in the three areas in terms of family structure (Table 1.1) and ethnic origin (Table 1.2).

Table 1.1: HOUSEHOLD TYPES IN THE INTERVIEW SURVEY

Household type	Single women	Couples
Pregnant women (no children)	0	5
With children under 5 years:		
1 child	17*	13
2 or more	1	3**
With children both under and over 5 years:		
2 children	4	5
3 or more	1	8
Total	23	34

*Includes one woman living with a woman friend and one pregnant woman
**Includes two pregnant women

The sample included eight pregnant women, three of whom already had children. While over half the families had just one child, there were 11 large families with six or more people. Altogether the families included 71 children under five: 20 of these were under one year old, with the rest fairly evenly spread between one and five years old. Women from a wide range of ethnic backgrounds were included, to reflect the homeless population as a whole.

Table 1.2: ETHNIC ORIGIN OF WOMEN IN THE SURVEY

Ethnic origin	Number
Afro Caribbean	7
African	3
Asian	10
Vietnamese	2
Irish	6
Other British/European	25
Others	4
Total	57

Table 1.3: ETHNIC ORIGIN AND HOUSEHOLD TYPE IN THE SURVEY

Household type	Afro-Carib & African	Asian & Vietnamese	Irish	Other British & European	Others	Total
Single woman — 1 child	6	0	1	8	1	16
Single woman — 2 or more children	2	0	0	4	0	6
Couple — woman pregnant	0	2	0	3	0	5
Couple — 1 child	2	2	1	6	2	13
Couple — 2 or more children	0	8	4	4	1	17
Total	10	12	6	25	4	57

Only seven of the women were under 20 years old, one third were in their early twenties, while a quarter were in their thirties. By focusing on those with children or pregnant most, but not all, had been placed in hotels by a local authority. The sample is therefore very different from one which would be designed to represent all hotel residents, including single people and childless couples.

The interviews

The interview, using a structured questionnaire (see Appendix 1) usually took between one and one and a half hours and in most cases was carried out in the hotel. No more than four women were interviewed in any one hotel, in most cases only one. Most interviews were conducted in English, with seven in Sylheti, two in Vietnamese and one in Spanish. Interviewing was done between June 1986 and early 1987, and all the interviewers were women.

During the interview the women were asked about their circumstances, their own and their children's health, their access to health services and reactions to living in bed and breakfast accommodation for a long period of time. Information on cooking facilities was also obtained and most of those interviewed were asked in detail about their own food and eating patterns. A small amount of information was also gathered about the children's diet.

Interviews with professionals

A range of professionals working regularly with families in hotels were interviewed personally. Discussions took place with midwives, health visitors, general practitioners and environmental health officers. The interviews were relatively unstructured and the intention was to allow the participants to express their feelings and describe their experiences in as uninhibited a way as possible.

Midwives and health visitors

Health visitors were contacted through the National Health Visitors Homeless Group, which involves those who work closely with or are concerned about homeless families. Interviews were conducted with members of the group and their colleagues in all three study areas. Midwives in the study areas were identified through the health visitors.

General practitioners

In London interviews were undertaken with GPs in Bayswater, Finsbury Park, and Hounslow. In Manchester the one GP who was interviewed had a practice that was close to a hotel used by homeless families — but not the closest. Other GPs in Manchester who were known not to accept the hotel homeless were unwilling to be interviewed for this study. The GP interviewed in Southend had recently moved to the practice close to the area with a high concentration of hotels but he could only recall having see between five and ten homeless patients in the previous six months.

Environmental health officers

Given the concern with standards and conditions expressed by health workers and the homeless themselves, environmental health officers in London, Southend and Manchester were asked how they tackled conditions in hotels in their authorities. In London the study focused on environmental health officers in two areas with high concentrations of homeless people in hotels: Camden and Westminster. The latter has nearly 5,000 HMOs, many of which are hotels.

Examination of health records

Using health records

Health records are intended to ensure smooth running health services by keeping a continuous record for each person using the services, and highlighting information which is believed to be most useful in the person's health care. Infant health records, for example, give details of the child's birthweight and immunisation status. But these records, like the health services themselves, are designed for a stable population.

Homeless families often have frequent changes of address, requiring numerous amendments to medical cards which can sometimes lead to misdirected appointment letters. Many of the families have previously lived with a series of friends or relations, or in short-term lets, and moved from bed and breakfast hotels to stay with family or friends only to return to another hotel. Changes of surname when single mothers move into a relationship and take their partner's name can also cause confusion and duplication of records.

Medical records generally detail only incidents of ill-health which lead the patient to consult a GP or attend a hospital. However, because of the importance to long-term health of good health in pregnancy and the first months of life, mothers and babies have access to some of the few preventive health services available in this country. Maternity and infant health records should include information not just about illnesses and health problems, but also about positive health measures, such as immunisations, and about routine developmental assessments, which can pick up at an early stage handicap or delay in a baby's development.

Homeless families can make enormous demands on health workers for support and advice on obtaining housing, benefits, play facilities and schooling for their children. These demands can mean that detailed recording of health issues may not be given the highest priority and only the barest information may be routinely recorded in the health records.

The areas included
The part of the study concerned with health records

was carried out only in London and Manchester, where there were sizeable concentrations of homeless families. Nearly a third of homeless families come from London boroughs, and they are concentrated in certain areas where there are numerous bed and breakfast hotels. City and Hackney District Health Authority includes such an area of concentration, and the authority has given considerable thought to the way in which services can best be organised to reach homeless families. City and Hackney runs a mobile health clinic to service its homeless families. The clinic records provided a ready-made population of homeless families with children for this study. Control groups for comparison with the homeless children were drawn from the same authority and from Tower Hamlets Health Authority.

In Manchester, the majority of homeless families are in South Manchester District Health Authority. South Manchester, too, has considered the needs of its homeless families, and a special steering group meets regularly to discuss services for them. It brings together representatives of the health authority, the housing and social services departments, and relevant voluntary organisations. A number of specialist health workers for homeless families are employed by the authority, but the families' records are not kept separate from those of other families, nor are they easily identifiable.

In City and Hackney, Tower Hamlets and South Manchester permission for the study was obtained first from the relevant ethical committee and then from senior health staff, who also provided invaluable support and information as well as introductions to medical records departments and to health visitors responsible for the children in the study.

The analysis of health records

The health measures examined in this study included: problems recorded in pregnancy, babies' birthweight, immunisations and developmental assessments. Indicators were chosen which were most likely to be routinely recorded and, as far as possible, where comparative data for families who were not homeless was available.

In London infant health records were looked at, and a series of control groups were built into the London study for comparative purposes. A copy of the data collection sheets used appears in Appendix 2. In Manchester, permission was given to examine obstetric and infant health records of homeless families. Data from these was generally compared with district or national data on the same measures of health.

In constructing the homeless samples in London and Manchester, babies were included only if they had been living in bed and breakfast accommodation for at least three months (this could include some months of the mother's pregnancy). A number of the children had moved in and out of hotels several times in their short lives, but they were included in the sample only if they were under two years old when they last moved into bed and breakfast accommodation.

In London, the health records held at the mobile clinic in Hackney provided a sample of infants currently living in hotels. When those who had been there for less than three months were excluded, the sample consisted of 41 children born and still living in bed and breakfast accommodation (called here the "born and bred" sample), and 49 born outside hotels who had moved in during 1985 and 1986 (called here the "moved in" sample). Because homeless families are known to include many who suffer other disadvantages — single mothers, unskilled and unemployed people, recent immigrants and ethnic minority families — information was also collected for two control groups who came from a similar background. By comparing children in homeless families with others who shared many of the same family characteristics, the effect of homelessness itself should become clearer. One control group matched for age and sex with the born and bred sample were drawn from the same clinic from which the homeless families' mobile clinic operated (the Hackney sample). A second control group came from clinics in Tower Hamlets, another London borough serving a population with a similar ethnic and social class mix to that of the homeless families (the Tower Hamlets sample).

In Manchester, the Homeless Families Department of the City Council provided access to information on homeless families who had been rehoused from hotels in South Manchester during 1988, and 42 records were traced.

Starting from a list of 116 households on the Council's register of families moving in and out of homeless families' accommodation, mothers and babies were lost from the sample at every subsequent stage. Given the pressure on homeless families departments and on the health services catering for them, it is not surprising if record-keeping is not always a top priority, but the number of losses on the way to the final sample is remarkable. Over half of the original households were lost even before the search of health records began, the majority of them simply untraceable. This reflects the high degree of mobility amongst homeless families. It is quite likely that some of those rehoused in 1986 were homeless again by 1987, and that this was why their files were not available; others had almost certainly moved outside Manchester. The difficulty in tracking down mothers and children who had been living in bed and breakfast accommodation tells us almost as much about their relationship to health services as does the content of their health records.

The mothers and children

All the children in the London and Manchester samples were under two years old when they moved into bed and breakfast accommodation and all had either spent at least three months in a hotel themselves, or their mothers had spent at least three months of the pregnancy in one.

Babies born and bred in hotels tended, not surprisingly, to be younger than those who moved in some time after the birth, but two had been living in hotels for close to two years and a third for more than 12 months. Half the babies who moved into bed and breakfast accommodation were also less than one year old. Overall, large numbers of very young children in homeless families spend their early formative months living in a hotel room.

In Manchester a quarter of the homeless mothers were rehoused before or on the birth of their baby in line with the Council's policy, which attempted to avoid putting new babies into hotels. Nevertheless, six of the children in the sample had lived in bed and breakfast accommodation for at least three months before they were six months old.

An attempt was made to establish what percentage of the homeless infants were of Asian origin, because it was known that Bangladeshi families, in particular, were seriously over-represented amongst families in bed and breakfast accommodation in London. Because the infant health record does not show the mother's place of birth, the only accessible ethnic identification was from the child's surname, and this was therefore used. It is recognised that this is an unsatisfactory measure in many ways since it is based only on the father's name and it does not, for example, distinguish between British-born Asians, East African Asians and those born on the Indian sub-continent (Table 1.4).

Table 1.4: PERCENTAGE OF INDIAN, BANGLADESHI AND PAKISTANI CHILDREN INCLUDED IN THE RECORDS ANALYSIS

	London sample %	Manchester sample %
Born and bred	80	7
Moved in	30	
Hackney	12	
Tower Hamlets	88	

In London, eight out of ten of the homeless children born in hotels were from an Asian background, compared with three out of ten children who moved into bed and breakfast accommodation after birth. The Hackney control sample included a much smaller proportion with Asian names, but the Tower Hamlets group provides a useful comparison on questions where ethnic background may be significant. Only three (seven per cent) of the Manchester sample of homeless families were of Asian origin.

The minimum length of stay in a hotel was three months. Precise information about length of stay was not collected in London. However, the ages of the born and bred sample indicate the minimum period for which they had already lived in hotels. The average age was ten months and, as noted above, some children in this group had already spent nearly two years in such accommodation. The picture was quite different in Manchester. None of the children in the Manchester sample had been in a bed and breakfast hotel for longer than 12 months, the average stay being six months.

REFERENCES

1   "Homelessness Statistics", *DOE Quarterly.*
2   *Ibid.*
3   Andrew D. Thomas with Alan Hedges, *The 1985 Physical and social survey of houses in multiple occupation in England and Wales,* DOE, HMSO. 1986.
4   Judith Littlewood and Anthea Tinker, *Families in flats.* DOE, HMSO. 1981.
Dr James Dunlop, "A doctor looks at housing", *Housing Magazine,* Vol 16 No 3 March 1980.
Pearl Jephcott, *Young Families in high flats,* City of Birmingham Housing Dept. 1977.
Pearl Jephcott, *Homes in high flats,* Oliver and Boyd. 1971.
5   Geoffrey Randall, Denise Francis and Catriona Brougham, *A place for the*

family, SHAC. 1981
Speaking for ourselves, Bayswater Homeless Project. 1987.
Ed. Alan Murie and Syd Jeffers, "Living in bed and breakfast: the experience of homelessness in London", Working Paper No. 71, Bristol School for Advanced Urban Studies. 1987.

6   *No place like home.* West London Homelessness Group.
7   P. Townsend and N. Davidson, *Inequalities in Health: The Black Report,* Pelican edition, Penguin. 1982.
Margaret Whitehead, *The Health Divide: inequalities in health in the 1980s,* Health Education Council. March 1987.
8   "Deprivation and ill health." British Medical Association Board of Science and Education Discussion Paper. May 1982.
9   Editorial in the *The Lancet.* August 1986.
10   Isobel Cole-Hamilton and Tim Lang, *Tightening belts: a report on the impact of poverty on food,* The London Food Commission. June 1986.
11   P. Townsend and N. Davidson, *op.cit.*
12   *English House Condition Survey, Part 2,* DOE, HMSO. 1981.
13   "A survey of families in bed and breakfast hotels". Valerie Howarth, Report to the Thomas Coram Foundation for Children. April-June 1987.
14   Barbara Saunders, *Homeless young people in Britain — the contribution of the voluntary sector,* ERICA and DSU. 1986.
15   "Primary health care for homeless single people in London: a strategic approach", Report of the Health sub-group of the Joint Working Party on Single Homelessness in London. January 1987.
16   "Health visitors and homeless families", *Health Visitors Journal.* November 1986.
Jonathan Stearn, "An expensive way of making children ill", *Roof* Magazine. September/October 1986.

Mike Abrahams/Network.

Homeless family living in bed and breakfast accomodation. Bayswater, London 1986.

CHAPTER 2
Conditions in bed and breakfast hotels

Introduction and summary

HOTELS HAVE NOW become a new form of housing for many homeless people. Many children know no other home. The interviews with the women show the appalling standards and conditions of this expanding form of housing. The high level of stress and illness found amongst the families interviewed is likely to be a reflection of the inadequacy of the accommodation.

Visits to hotels spread across London, Manchester and Southend provided a catalogue of the conditions in which many homeless families have to live. In these circumstances even small problems can become major irritants as the weeks and months go by.

Most of the families had to share the WC and bathroom with several others and a significant number shared with ten or more other people. Many had an unreliable supply of hot water and heating and found the hotel dirty and unhygienic. Very few of the women in the survey had access to reasonable cooking facilities, and many even had problems keeping food. Six women had no means of preparing basic food or even making a hot drink.

There was considerable concern amongst the women about the safety of the accommodation. These fears for safety are not misplaced. In the last few years there have been a number of fires in hotels in which people have died, and in July 1987 a child died falling from a fourth-floor window in a hotel in London. People living in bed and breakfast hotels have no sense of security and this exacerbates the stresses of living there.

Hotels are often noisy, and many women complained of the lack of privacy: several said it was "like a prison". One woman described how restricting it was to have to sit in the dark in the evenings when the youngest child was asleep as there was nowhere to go.

The study found extremely high levels of overcrowding. Nearly half the households were estimated as being over the legal standards for crowding. Many of the children had to share their bed, sometimes with an adult, and the bedrooms often had no space for a table or chairs.

The conditions found in many of the hotels surveyed would be difficult to cope with for even a short period: yet the women in this study had generally been living in hotels for some considerable time with nearly a third having lived in hotels for a year or more. Most thought they would be there at least another year or said they had no idea how long it might be before they were rehoused. There was a widespread lack of information or understanding of their position: they often felt dumped and abandoned by the council. Health visitors were also worried about the poor conditions in hotels but felt unable to put pressure on the councils to act.

The families in this study had very little money to spend. Most were unemployed and those in work were earning very low wages. Yet hotel life is itself expensive and many families were having to go without basic necessities including food.

Amenities

MOST HOUSEHOLDS in the survey had to share the WC and the bath or shower. Eleven shared with ten or more people (Table 2.1). For a quarter of the households the WC was on another floor of the hotel, and similarly, for a quarter the bath or shower was on another floor. It is easy in a private house to go up or down stairs to the WC or bathroom. But in a hotel — where there is little privacy, where it is not safe to leave young children alone in the bedroom, where the room may have to be locked every time it is left, and where there may well be a queue for the WC or bathroom — having no facilities on the same floor is extremely inconvenient. Over a third of the women interviewed said that the hot water supply in the bath or shower was not constant: in one case there was no hot water available at all.

While nearly all the households had exclusive use of a washbasin, a third had only an irregular supply of hot water.

Table 2.1: ACCESS TO AMENITIES IN THE SURVEY

	WC	Bath or shower
Exclusive use	16	21
Sharing with 1-4 other people	8	7
Sharing with 5-9 other people	12	9
Sharing with 10-19 other people	10	7
Sharing with 20 or more people	1	4
Don't know	10	9
Total women interviewed	57	57

Heating and hygiene

When it is the only room to live in, conditions in the bedroom are crucial. Nearly two-thirds of the women said the heating in their room was not satisfactory in some way: usually the room was too cold. Having no control over the heating, and the room being too hot or stuffy were also common problems. A third of the rooms suffered from general dampness, damp patches or mould.

Over a third of the women were concerned about cleanliness in the hotel. The most commonly mentioned problems were dirty

WCs and bathrooms, bad smells, and the presence of fleas, cockroaches and other bugs. In at least four hotels the management did not even clean the common areas and the residents had to buy materials and clean the WCs, bathrooms and halls themselves. Eleven women found rubbish disposal a problem, with bags having to be kept in the bedroom or left in the hallways, sometimes for days. The women were most concerned about the smells and hygiene, but rubbish left lying about also poses a serious fire risk. One woman commented about the hotel in which she was living: "They should burn it down. It's disgusting."

Food

The storage, preparation and cooking of food are all likely to play an important part in determining what kinds of food women in bed and breakfast accommodation eat (see also Chapter 5). The women were therefore asked for details of the facilities available to them and how often they used them.

Storing food

Food storage was found to be a major problem for most of the women. Some hotels did not allow residents to keep any food in their rooms, and keeping perishable food was a common difficulty. Most women felt there was insufficient space for storing food. Only eight felt they had no problems. All but one of these eight had a fridge in their bedroom, and three also had a cupboard (see Table 2.2). The presence of a fridge or cupboard in the bedroom did not necessarily mean there were no problems, and even the majority of women with these facilities were unhappy in some way about the food storage provision.

Nearly half the women did not have a fridge either in their room or elsewhere. Ten did not even have a cupboard in the bedroom where food could be kept. While some tried to keep food cool on the windowsill, six said they could keep no food at all. Two

Table 2.2: FOOD STORAGE SPACE USED BY THE WOMEN IN THE SURVEY

Food storage space	Number of women
Cupboard in bedroom	30
Fridge in bedroom	23
Other space in bedroom	10
Fridge in kitchen	7
Windowsill	7
Cupboard in kitchen	5
Total women interviewed	57

women with babies of three and four months, who wanted to start weaning, felt that they were unable to start giving them solid food because there was nowhere to keep it. Ten said they had problems with cockroaches or other bugs (see Table 2.3).

Table 2.3: PROBLEMS EXPERIENCED IN STORING FOOD IN THE SURVEY

Nature of problem	Number of women reporting problems
Food goes off	15
No fridge	12
Space too small	12
Cockroaches, bugs etc.	10
Food gets stolen	2
Space is dirty	1
Other	15
Total women interviewed	57

Preparing food

Most women (41 out of the 57) had some difficulties with preparing food. The major problem for many women was that there was nowhere for food preparation at all. Twenty-three of the 57 women reported this. Seven said the area available was too dangerous, seven said it was too far away, and four women said it was too dirty. Women were especially concerned about having to use knives in the bedroom where young children could hurt themselves.

Cooking and kitchens

Access to kitchens and cooking facilities is crucially important to hotel residents. The Association of London Authorities has a code of practice for kitchen facilities in hotels for homeless families. According to this, one full set of kitchen facilities should be available for every five people and should not be more than one floor away. One full set of facilities includes an oven, four burners, a grill, a sink, a fridge and storage facilities. In this survey only four women had facilities which met the standards given in the ALA code of practice.

Only five of the 57 families in this survey had exclusive use of a kitchen. Twenty-two had no kitchen they could use at all. The rest shared a kitchen with at least three other families, and many shared with large numbers: in six cases over 20 families had to share the kitchen (see Table 2.4). This was a major problem for many of the women. There seemed to be little relationship between the facilities provided in shared kitchens and the number of families expected to share them. For example, one kitchen had only six rings for over 20 families, while another had just four rings for over 30 families to use.

The 35 women in hotels where there were kitchens were asked whether or not they actually used them. Despite a number of difficulties and widespread dissatisfaction, only seven women did

Table 2.4: KITCHEN FACILITIES AVAILABLE TO THE WOMEN IN THE SURVEY

Kitchen facilities	Number of women
Exclusive use	5
Share kitchen with 3-4 other families	5
Share kitchen with 6-7 other families	4
Share kitchen with 11-19 other families	5
Share kitchen with 20 or more families	6
Share kitchen with unknown no. of others	10
No kitchen	22
Total	57

not. The shared kitchens were often a long way from the bedrooms, two-thirds were two or more floors away, and many of the women were concerned about having to carry hot food, pots and pans up and down the stairs. Several women also said food and pans tended to get stolen from the kitchen if left for even a brief time. In one hotel children were not allowed in the kitchen, but the woman interviewed felt she could not leave them alone in the bedroom either.

Those women without access to a kitchen did not necessarily have facilities in their rooms, and six women had no means of preparing even a hot drink; there was no kitchen, and not even a kettle in their room. Most of the women did have a kettle in their room although 13 did not. Some women had limited cooking facilities in their room such as rings, a grill or an oven, but these were often very small and belonged to the families themselves. A few women had their own toasters, sandwich-makers or electric pans. Several women said they did not like having to cook in their rooms because it was dangerous with small children around. One woman was very concerned about the safety of having a kettle in the bedroom when she reported: "My daughter and baby have burnt themselves. They try to pull the plug out."

It is clear from this survey that most hotels do not cater for people providing meals for themselves. Some homeless families live in hotels for long periods of time and have to make use of whatever facilities exist, however inadequate. Problems with preparing, storing and cooking food are common, and as a result many families find they cannot eat the kind of food they would like. This was especially true for those women who did not have a kitchen they could use, and who relied most on take-aways and cafes.

Safety and security

Physical safety

A specific worry for many women in hotels is the lack of safety. Forty-four of the 57 women interviewed felt their hotel was not a safe place. Women from ethnic minorities were much more likely than white British women to feel the hotel was not safe. The women were concerned both about physical dangers in the hotels and about the lack of privacy and control within the hotels.

Physical safety problems which worried the women included the danger of children falling out of windows or through broken balcony or stair rails, young children playing in halls and stairways and in cramped rooms, kettles and cooking equipment in bedrooms, and bad or inadequate electrical wiring with open fuse boxes, adaptors and trailing wires. One family had resorted to putting a wardrobe in front of their insecure fourth-floor window to prevent the children from falling out.

Fire risks

Twenty-four of the 57 women said the fire alarms did not work properly: in some cases they had never heard them ring, while in others they seemed to ring frequently with no cause —

which encouraged people to ignore them. Three women said that there were no fire alarms at all, while in one hotel where they were regularly tested, the bell had failed to ring when there actually was a fire. While most hotels had a telephone which residents could use, eight did not: in these hotels it would be difficult to contact the emergency services quickly.

Security

In addition to these physical problems in hotels, many women felt the hotels were not safe because of the lack of privacy and lack of control over common areas. Several said there were strangers, drunks or prostitutes in the corridors. Burglaries from the rooms seemed quite a common fear; the hotel front door was often left open, allowing strangers in and children out. In one hotel the manager would use his keys to come into the rooms unannounced, while in another an older boy had gone into a bedroom and attacked a three-month-old sleeping baby, who then needed hospital treatment.

Overcrowding in hotel rooms

A couple and their four children, aged from one to six, lived in a basement room approximately 10 feet by 17 feet. With the two double beds pushed together, the sink, wardrobe and chest of drawers, there was little space left for the possessions of a family of six.

While conditions in hotels vary greatly, most would not be comfortable to stay in for even a short period of time. For families with young children who must live there for many months or even years, the most striking problem in this survey was lack of space.

Where possible, the interviewer estimated the size of the bedroom. Where this was done over a third of the rooms were estimated to be under 110 square feet (the equivalent of a room 10 feet by 11 feet). These were mostly occupied by two people (a couple or single parent with one child), but there were five families in the survey where three people had to live in a room of this size. Larger families did tend to have larger rooms, and some of the very large families had two rooms. However, two families, each with two adults and four children, were estimated to be living in less than 220 square feet altogether (the equivalent of one room under 14 feet by 16 feet).

It is possible to compare the space available to the households in this survey with the statutory definition of overcrowding. This is based on a "person standard" which measures anyone over ten years old as one person and a child of one to nine as half a person: babies under one are not counted. Each household, measured by this "person standard", is required to have a minimum number of square feet of living space. In addition, households with a "person standard" of over 2P should have at least two rooms and those with over 4P should have at least three rooms.

The households in this study have been measured under this "person standard" and Table 2.5 relates this to the amount of space they occupy.

Of the 42 households where details were obtained, nearly half were statutorily overcrowded: 15 were overcrowded because they did not have enough space and a further five had enough space, but failed to meet the statutory standard because they only had one room and should have had two. Nine of these 20 households were overcrowded under both measures.

"You feel the walls closing in on you"

Table 2.5: OVERCROWDING IN THE SURVEY

Size of households in the survey (measured in "person standard")	Under 90	91-110	111-160	161-180	181-200	201-220	221-270	271+	NK	TOTAL
1p	2	1	1						3	7
1½p		7	2		1					10
2p	2	2	3	2			1		3	13
2½p	1	1	4					1	3	10
3p			1	1			2			4
3½p						1	1		1	3
4p			1		1	1	1		3	7
5p									1	1
6p						1				1
6½p									1	1
Total	5	11	11	4	1	1	6	3	15	57

▢ shows where the households are overcrowded in terms of space

■ shows where the households are overcrowded because they do not have enough rooms

Many of the bedrooms were clearly inadequate for the number of people living there and their possessions. There was often no room for furniture other than beds and a cupboard: many families had no table or chair. There was often insufficient space for each person to have a bed. Of the 110 children of all ages in the families, at least 33 were sharing their bed with another child and 13 had to share with an adult. Some rooms were too small even for a baby's cot. One child just had a mattress on the floor while another had a fold-up bed which, when open, fitted across the entrance to the room. Bigger families tended to have more children sharing with each other, while sharing with an adult was equally common where there was a single parent with one child. Two families, each with two adults and four children, had just two double beds for all six people.

This survey has shown a remarkable level of overcrowding amongst homeless hotel residents. Where the information was obtained nearly half the households were statutorily overcrowded, with some families living considerably below the standard. This, coupled with the isolation felt by many of the mothers and the large amount of time many spend in their rooms each day, must put immense pressure on the families.

How long families stay in hotels

While most of the women in the interview sample had been placed in their hotels by a local authority, seven had not. In one case the council had accepted only a temporary responsibility to place the household in a hotel, and did not regard itself as having a duty to rehouse the family. The families had been placed in their hotels by 12 different councils including nine London boroughs.

"The council originally said one to two months. Then they said six months. Now they won't say how long."

People who had been in bed and breakfast hotels for only a short period were not included in the sample. For those interviewed, the length of time they had been living in bed and breakfast accommodation varied. Some had been there for more than two years (Table 2.6)

The sample of homeless families whose health records were analysed presents a similar picture. Of babies under two years old who were born, and who were still living in hotels in London,

Table 2.6: TIME SPENT IN HOTELS SO FAR, IN THE SURVEY

Length of time	Number of women
4-5 months	15
6-11 months	24
1-2 years	14
Over 2 years	4
Total	57

for example, a third had been there for more than a year. Although the longer-term hotel residents were less likely to be any council's responsibility than those there for shorter periods, 12 women who were awaiting council rehousing had already been living in hotels for over a year. There was a clear tendency for Asian families to have longer residence in hotels than white families; this may be partly explained by the fact that larger families tend to stay longer.

Previous research has shown that people's feelings about where they live are likely to be affected by how long they think they might be there.[1] Three-quarters of the women thought they might have to stay at least another year in the hotel or said they had no idea how long it would be before they were rehoused. Most of the remainder thought they would be there up to another six months. Women from ethnic minorities were most likely to say they had no idea how much longer they might be there, perhaps reflecting the fact that they seem more likely to have to stay for longer, coupled with a general lack of understanding of why they had been put in a hotel in the first place. This particularly applied to the eight Bangladeshi women in the survey.

Many of the women interviewed felt that the council was not keeping them adequately informed of their position. Several said the council officer they had originally dealt with had left and they did not have a new contact person; it was often difficult to get through on the telephone; messages left were not responded to; when they did finally talk to someone in the council they felt they were being "fobbed off". Their general sense of having been dumped in a hotel and forgotten made it harder to cope with the conditions they were having to live in, and is likely to have exacerbated their stress and anxiety.

> "I came across a family from Rochford in a hotel. I phoned up the homeless persons officer and asked him why he had not notified us. The man said they had enough paperwork to do, thank you very much. I asked how long they would be there and he told me they would be out as soon as possible but would not give any time period. I asked him where they would be going to, so that I could forward their records. At that point he shut me up by saying that 'I know you have got your job to do but these families are well able to look after themselves, they do not need you.' And that was that."
> Comment from one of the health visitors interviewed

Employment

"The Job Centre were going to put my husband on a Job Start Scheme but told him not to bother until we get a flat."

Living in a bed and breakfast hotel imposes many pressures on health, mental state and on social and family life. Not only are most homeless families in a poor economic position when they become homeless, but living in a hotel itself makes it harder to get work.

Only nine of the 57 women in this study either had a job themselves or had a partner with a job. The jobs they had were low paid. Those with jobs found that their work was affected by living in a hotel, largely because the hotel charges were too high in relation to their wages, even with housing benefit. One husband, for example, had to work a large amount of overtime to cover the costs of the hotel. Life in a hotel also made it difficult to hold a job for other reasons: one working husband found the hotel too noisy to get a good night's sleep, while another working woman found she was having to take a large amount of time off work with migraine. Two of those working also pointed out that their employers could not easily and quickly get in touch with them, for example to arrange overtime working.

A few in this survey had previously had a job, but had given it up when they moved to the hotel. This was because bills had taken too much out of their wages, the journey to work had become too difficult, or they were too tired or stressed to keep the job.

While most of the mothers in the survey were not looking for work because they had young children to look after, most of the partners were hoping to get a job eventually. However living in a hotel made this very difficult. The main reason was, again, that if they got a job they would then have to pay towards the hotel bills out of their wages: with the level of wages they were likely to earn this would be financially crippling. In some cases the hotel was felt to be too unsafe to leave the woman and children alone all day, and this deterred partners from looking for work. Several partners said that as soon as they moved into a flat they would be able to take a job. Two women said they would like to get work as soon as they were rehoused and could settle their children into child care.

Money

The high level of unemployment in the sample and the low wages of those working left most families very short of money.

Table 2.7 below shows the remaining weekly disposable income of the households in the survey (including those with wage earners and those without) *after* hotel charges had been paid. The research was mostly done in late 1986 and early 1987. Most single women lived on under £70 a week while none had more than £130 a week. Couples were little better off, with more than half living on under £100 a week.

Table 2.7: INCOME AND TYPE OF HOUSEHOLD IN THE SURVEY

Remaining income after hotel costs have been paid (£)

Household type	Under 50	51-70	71-100	101-130	131-180	181+	Total
Single woman — one child	6	8	1	—	—	—	15
Single woman — 2 or more children	1	—	3	2	—	—	6
Couple pregnant or with 1 child	3	3	7	—	3	—	16
Couple — 2 or more children	—	—	3	2	2	3	10
Total	10	11	14	4	5	3	47

Living in a hotel is more expensive than living in normal housing for a number of reasons: buying take-away food or food in small quantities as it cannot be stored, is expensive; relying on launderettes for all clothes washing and drying is costly; families may often have to travel some distance to keep in touch with family or friends; there is also pressure to spend money on going out to escape from the cramped conditions.

The women were asked if there was anything they had to go without because they could not afford it. Well over half said they could not buy clothes and shoes for themselves and a slightly smaller number said they could not afford the clothes and shoes they needed for their children either. Nearly a third said they went without food themselves, while six said they could not afford enough food for their children. Other studies of poverty and food have also found that where money is short it is the mothers who go without in order to feed the rest of the family. One woman interviewed for this survey said she sometimes went without food for a couple of days. Many also mentioned their inability to buy toys and equipment for the children and the fact that they could not afford trips out. As one woman put it, "people don't realise how much it costs to live in a place like this."

> "The council pays £117.10 a week for my room. It would be better to give the money direct to me so that I could find somewhere decent. The landlords are rich at the expense of the poor people."

People in bed and breakfast hotels generally have financial as well as housing problems. Hotel life is expensive, most of those living in them are unemployed, and those who have jobs tend to have low wages. Yet living in a hotel itself makes it difficult to get work, and people find themselves in an "unemployment trap", where they would not be able to afford to live in the hotel if they took work. The disposable incomes of those in this study were extremely low and people were having to go without basic necessities. Nearly a third of the women were sometimes going without food. The lack of money is likely to affect the health of hotel residents both by increasing their worries and by restricting their diet.

Local authority action on standards

"If I had a chance I wouldn't let pigs live here. No-one from the council has been to see the room."

Several women interviewed in the study pointed out that no-one from the council had been to see their room since they had been living there, and felt that perhaps no-one knew what it was like. In one area there was a feeling that the council only placed people in the worst local hotels.

The health visitors interviewed also had strong feelings about the role and activities of local authorities in monitoring bed and breakfast hotels. They believed that proper concern for the health of homeless families should include seeking to improve the standards and conditions in hotels. However they are in a difficult position. If environmental health officers do not inspect the hotel and take action to improve conditions, some of the health visitors felt they had to press the council to act. Yet that may well compromise the good relationship they need with hotel managers if they are to gain access to homeless families.

In Southend one of the health visitors explained that when she contacts the environmental health office about standards in particular hotels, the officers complain that they have not got enough staff to inspect. This health visitor related a story to indicate the lengths she has to go to get the environmental health department to take action. "I went to do a new birth visit in a bedsit, where there was a young woman and her baby and five other single women. Some cowboys had put in an electric meter that was smoking. When the residents complained, the landlord gave them a fire extinguisher and told them not to use it unless they really had to, as the insurance would cover any damage. I phoned the environmental health who said they had a backlog of work and were not going to act very quickly. So I made an anonymous phone call to the fire brigade who then made the environmental health department close the basement down."

A health visitor in Finsbury Park had a similar story. "I went to visit a seven-day-old baby in a hotel where the ceiling had collapsed while the family were in bed. You could see the furniture hanging through from the room upstairs. Yet the environmental health office refused to close the place down. They also refused to take any action against another hotel annexe that had a shower in the kitchen with sewage coming up through the waste pipe."

Even in Manchester, where health visitors and environmental health officers meet each other in a steering group, the health visitors are not completely happy with the action taken by environmental health officers. A health visitor explained "Environmental health have served notices on a hotel that everyone agrees should really be closed down. Bits and pieces of work get done, but it's never going to have decent standards and conditions. As the housing department is desperate for places, the environmental health department is forced to compromise and the place is never going to get closed down."

The frustration of the health visitors when trying to get action on standards and conditions in hotels was reflected in a joint Health Visitors Association/Shelter survey.[2] Only three HVA centres had not encountered problems with living conditions in bed and breakfast hotels, yet only half the centres had sought help from environmental health officers.

REFERENCES

1   Geoffrey Randall, Denise Francis and Catriona Brougham, *A place for the family*, SHAC 1981.
2   "Health visitors and homeless families". *Health Visitors Journal*. November 1986.

CHAPTER 3

The health of homeless women in hotels

Introduction and summary

Sheila and her 14-month-old daughter live in a room approximately seven feet by 15 feet. The small window is at least six feet high up on the wall and gives very little light. As there is no room for a cot, the daughter shares Sheila's bed and disturbs her through the night. The hotel has no kitchen and food is not allowed in the rooms. Sheila does not even have a kettle to make a hot drink. She is often hungry, but worries more about her daughter who is often ill and does not seem to be growing.

> THE INTERVIEWS with women living in bed and breakfast hotels exposed a high incidence of illness. Many felt run down and tired and said their health was generally worse than before they had lived in a hotel. One of the most striking findings of the interview survey is the degree of stress experienced by the women. Depression and tension were common. Isolation was found to be a major problem. Hotel life also seemed to accentuate the tensions of family life and put great strains on relationships.
>
> GPs and health visitors were extremely concerned about both the physical and mental health of women in hotels. This study suggests that these women should be seen as amongst the most vulnerable in our society.

Physical health

THE INTERVIEWS with the women sought information about their health problems and any illnesses they had had since living in hotels. The most commonly mentioned ailments were severe headaches or migraines which 34 women said they had regularly; 20 women had had diarrhoea, usually with vomiting; 16 had suffered some kind of chest infection. Other problems often mentioned were bladder and kidney infections and anaemia. Two women said their asthma had got much worse since living in a hotel. Many women said they generally felt run down and tired and were more susceptible to coughs and colds. Well over half the women interviewed felt that their health was generally worse than before they had lived in a hotel, the rest saying their health had not changed. A third often took medicines or pills. One remark summed up the feelings of many: "I just don't bother about myself so much."

General practitioners expressed concern about the health of women they saw from bed and breakfast accommodation. The GP interviewed in Hounslow, who regularly visits a large hotel housing homeless families, compared their health with the health of his other 1,800 patients. He felt that homeless adults suffered from "more psychiatric problems, depression, anxiety and sleeplessness, and homeless children suffer from more upper respiratory tract infections. Infections do spread around the hotel — gastro-enteritis is common and we have had an outbreak of measles and chickenpox. But these have been reduced since the vaccination clinic was started. Having said that, homeless people are more likely to come to me if they have an infection. There is a higher consultation rate amongst the homeless than other patients."

Many of the women's health problems could be related specifically to their poor living conditions (see Chapter 2). For example those normally confined in their room for eight or more hours during the day were much more likely to have been ill (especially with diarrhoea and vomiting) than those who were normally out more. One woman, whose nearest kitchen was on the floor above, found that going up and down stairs affected her asthma. Burns and scalds from kettles and cooking rings sometimes resulted from the necessity to use such equipment in cramped bedrooms.

The standards of hygiene in the hotels was also related to the incidence of illness. Half the women interviewed said the WC and bathroom were dirty, and of them, nearly half had had diarrhoea and vomiting or other illnesses since living there.

The high incidence of illness amongst the women interviewed may be partly a product of the poor physical conditions in the hotels and partly a reflection of the high level of stress they experienced while living there. Being ill makes it even more difficult to cope.

> One mother of three young children, having lived in a hotel for over six months, was so desperate that she was afraid she might batter her children. She called the Social Services Department but they were unable to send a social worker to help.

Mental health

One of the most important findings of this survey is the degree of stress experienced by the women. In general women bear the major burden of hotel life and take the greatest responsibility for looking after children. Fathers are more often out at work than mothers and some women have no partners. Both those women with and those without partners in this survey seem to have suffered a high level of stress and depression since moving to a hotel.

The women were asked if they had experienced certain problems related to stress: a very high proportion had, as shown in Table 3.1.

Table 3.1: WOMEN'S SYMPTOMS OF STRESS

Unhappy most of the time	44
Tired most of the time	41
Often lose my temper	35
Often can't sleep at night	34
The children get on top of me	33
Burst into tears for no reason	24
Total women asked	56

Tension manifested itself in a number of ways: two women felt that they were very close to battering their children; two had started to drink heavily; one was losing weight rapidly despite the fact that she was still breastfeeding her baby. Many experienced severe depression and some had started to take pills to help.

> "It's very difficult when you've just split up from your husband. Going into a hotel makes it even worse."

Boredom, isolation and loneliness are among the main problems of those living in a hotel with small children. Nearly half the women in the survey, especially those with larger families, said they normally spent at least eight hours during the day in their bedroom, often not going out of the room at all except to the WC or bathroom. Overcrowding, with nearly half the households living in rooms which were below the statutory space standards, would accentuate the degree of stress felt by the women. (See Chapter 2.)

Some mothers may have been stuck in their rooms because of the practical problems of getting in and out with small children. Of the 11 families in rooms on the third floor or above, seven did not have a lift. These women, and those in hotels where the lift was often faulty, were more likely to spend most of the day in their rooms than those with better access.

> "I'm turning into a cabbage here. Sometimes I think I'm going mad in this box of a room."

The isolation of hotel life is also shown by the low level of social contact of many of the women interviewed. Many in the survey, especially those in London, were living some distance from their previous home area. Most of those who gave details had journeys of over half an hour to visit old friends or family and a quarter had a journey of over an hour. Over half the women said they saw less of other people to talk to since moving into a hotel. Many hotels wouldn't allow visitors to bedrooms.

On the other hand some women said they now saw more of other people because they had got to know others in the hotel, or were able to go to a playgroup or centre catering for homeless families. Those who did see more of other people were far less likely to feel unhappy and experience other problems than those who had reduced their level of social contact since moving to a hotel. Seeing other people can relieve some of the stresses of hotel life.

The health professionals felt that many of the health problems were related to the strain on the women of living in bed and breakfast hotels. One London GP saw the main problem for nearly all the families was "a pervasive sense of hopelessness, depression and despair. What you see are subtle changes in their health — more chest infections, more headaches and more anxiety." Although this GP could not say with complete confidence that these problems were solely related to hotel life, she felt that "anybody, no matter how happy and well balanced, who went into a hotel would suffer — physically and mentally."

Personal relationships

"It's very, very difficult to be living with each other all the time with no escape. It has affected our married life very much. We're not a couple any more."

Many women said that the stresses of living in a hotel had badly affected their relationships with their partners. One woman was on the point of breaking up with her husband at the time of the interview, but a week later had an offer of rehousing which she felt would save the marriage.

One midwife pointed to the straining of relationships between mothers and children when living in overcrowded conditions with new babies. But difficulties are not confined to the introduction of newborn babies into unsuitable, overcrowded hotel rooms. All the health visitors interviewed in Manchester, London and Southend expressed concern about stress and emotional problems affecting the whole family structure (see Chapters 4 and 6).

"When I am asked about families in hotels" said a health visitor in Manchester, "what I immediately think of is a mother who is apathetic and staying in bed till midday, with two children under five bouncing around in their cots. They have had no breakfast and are sitting around in a darkened smoky room, hungry, with no ventilation and no stimulation."

Several health care professionals, aware of the great amount of stress placed on parents, expressed surprise that the incidence of non-accidental injury to children was not higher than elsewhere. Hotel life, with isolation and overcrowding, seems to accentuate the tensions of family life and in some cases may threaten the family itself.

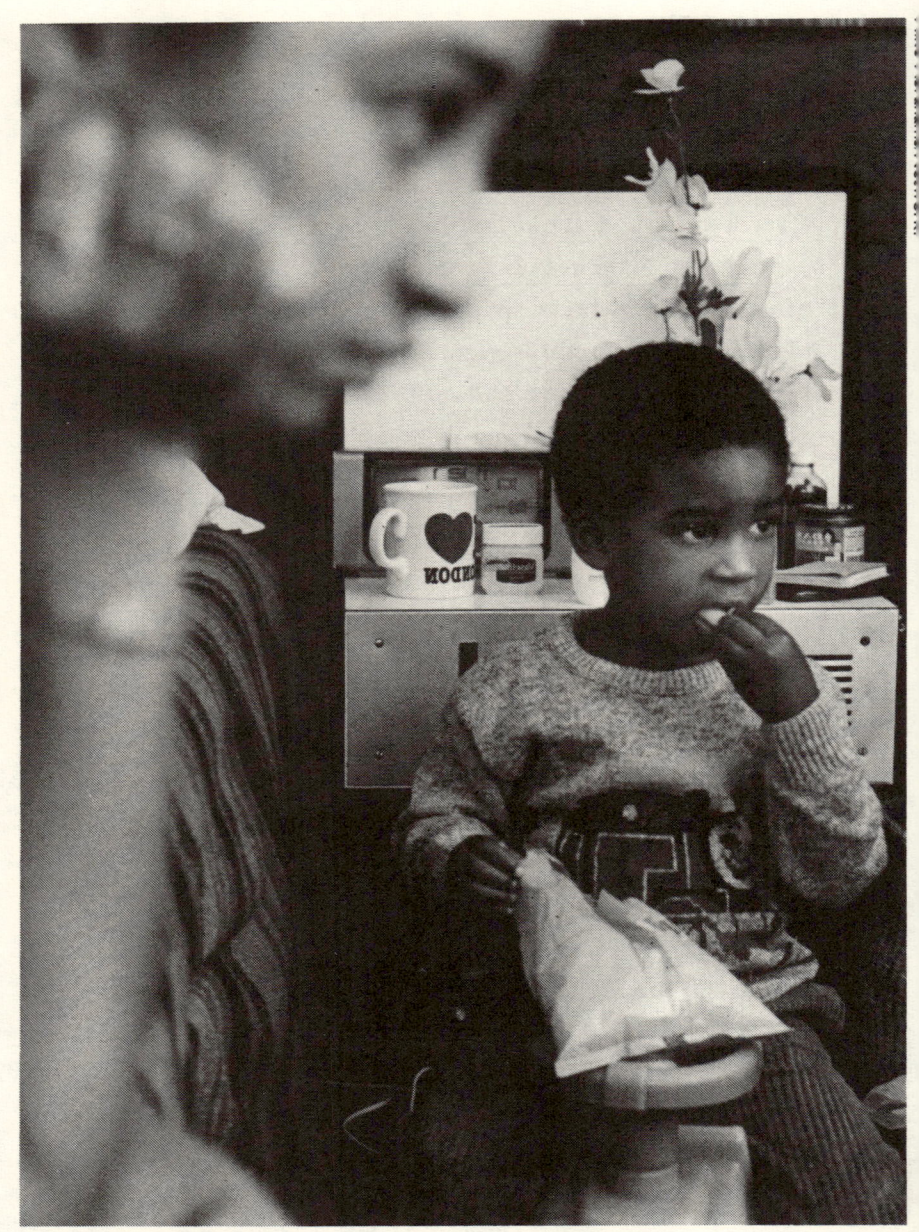

Homeless family living in bed and breakfast accomodation. Hounslow 1986.
The only play space for the children is in the hotel corridors.

CHAPTER 4
Hotel life for pregnant women

> **Introduction and summary**
>
> ALL THREE MAJOR areas of this study looked at the problems faced by homeless, pregnant women living in bed and breakfast accommodation. Such problems affect pregnant women and those with babies particularly acutely. The difficulty of getting proper meals, stress, noise levels and the lack of space can have a major impact in these circumstances. Three women in the interview survey volunteered that they would like to have more children but felt they could not while living in a hotel. Several of those with young babies were very anxious about how they could cope when the child started to crawl in a confined and potentially dangerous space.
> Health professionals were also found to be

> extremely concerned about the effects of living in bed and breakfast hotels on pregnant women. The study of health records shows these fears to be well founded: a larger number of health problems are recorded for pregnant women living in hotels than would normally be found.
>
> Hotel life jeopardises the health of all women. For those who are pregnant there is a grave risk to their health and the health of their babies. Chapter 6 looks at the problems of newborn babies in hotels: this chapter focuses on their mothers.

The women's own experiences

EIGHT WOMEN were pregnant at the time of the interview. Five said they were having problems with the pregnancy, including one who had a very long journey to her GP in the area she had previously lived, because she had not been able to find out where the local clinic was.

Nineteen of the children in the survey had been born while their mother was already living in bed and breakfast accommodation. Most of these mothers had moved into a hotel at least six months before the birth and half said they had had problems during the pregnancy. These included high blood pressure which the doctors had attributed to the stress of living in a hotel, and weight loss in one woman who had been unable to get proper meals in the hotel. Another woman had sometimes found it hard to walk in the later months of her pregnancy, and this had meant she often couldn't get to the kitchen, which was two floors from her bedroom.

Another woman said she had cried all through her pregnancy because she was upset about living in a hotel. For one, smoking had been a major problem, because she had been too stressed to give up, in spite of having given up smoking during two previous pregnancies when she had not been living in a hotel.

The women interviewed were very concerned about the welfare of their newborn babies in a hotel and were particularly worried about warmth and hygiene (see Chapter 6).

Jacqui, now with a child of 15 months who had lived nearly all his life in the hotel, said she sometimes wondered if she should have had an abortion instead, as "this was no life for him".

As well as those babies born to mothers already living in hotels, three more had been brought to a hotel as their first home. Their mothers described a range of problems they found when bringing a new baby back to a hotel, particularly the fact that the whole family was confined to one room, which was often too small to accommodate the baby as well. Noise was often a problem, either from the occupants of other rooms disturbing the baby or the baby disturbing other people. Some had difficulty keeping the new baby warm in the room. Several mentioned their concern about cockroaches and fleas in the hotel, mouldy carpets and the general level of dirt, and the difficulty of carrying a pram and baby up several flights of stairs to the bedroom where there was no lift in use.

Seven out of the 22 mothers who had brought a newborn baby to a hotel had had some health problems since the birth: four had not even gone for a post-natal check. One mother who haemorrhaged after the birth had been told "to relax", as it was all due to stress.

Pregnant women and diet

A good diet is crucially important for a pregnant woman. As Chapter 5 demonstrates, it is often very difficult to maintain a good diet when living in a bed and breakfast hotel because cooking facilities are so inadequate (see also Chapter 2). Some so-called "bed and breakfast" hotels don't even provide breakfast. Pregnant women are therefore particularly at risk of not getting an adequate diet.

Only five of the pregnant women in this survey gave information on their diet: three of them were assessed as having poor diets and two had average diets (see Chapter 5). The story of one of these women highlights the problem. She was seven and a half months pregnant at the time of the interview. She attended college and had to leave in the morning before the time when the hotel breakfast was served. Lunch was usually her first food of the day and she could only afford to buy snack food such as chips or a sandwich. The hotel had no cooking facilities of any kind for the residents to use. There was nowhere for storing food and milk could not be kept overnight in the heat of the bedroom. As a vegetarian she had a very limited choice from the local take-aways so her evening meal during the week normally consisted of chips and a milkshake, with an occasional pizza. Sometimes she just had biscuits and bread in the evenings. She did not even have a kettle in her room. She only had hot meals at weekends when she returned to her family in another part of London. This woman was desperately worried about her unborn baby because the doctors had told her that the baby's health was affected by her bad diet. She said, "I don't mind if I die, but if my baby dies what will I do?"

The views of health professionals

Health professionals were extremely concerned about the effects of living in bed and breakfast hotels on pregnant women. Midwives are in touch with women from twelve weeks into pregnancy up to four weeks after the birth. The midwives interviewed for this study felt that pregnant homeless women were often late booking into hospitals and had poor attendance at antenatal classes. One midwife was very unsympathetic towards those who did not maintain regular contact. However the health visitors recognised that it is often very difficult when women have moved into hotels after becoming pregnant. They have invariably booked with a hospital in the area where they became homeless and the main reason they do not change their booking to hospitals near the hotel is because they do not know how long they will be living there, or where they will move to next.

One midwife suggested that some homeless women were not as well motivated as others to attend antenatal clinics. But this may be because they are preoccupied with other difficulties, such as queueing at the DHSS, going to find out when they will be rehoused and visiting flats they have been offered.

All the midwives interviewed felt that homeless women and their unborn children were affected by the conditions they were living in. It was suggested that poor diets resulting from eating take-away food, meant that many homeless women suffered from anaemia and the growth of the foetus might be impaired. "If women go into labour and they are undernourished and anaemic," said one midwife,"any haemorrhaging would be more severe, and they become more anaemic."

"Because of their generally poor nutrition and poor standards of health, homeless women are more inclined to infections, post-partum haemorrhages and severe anaemia."

Overcrowding in a poor environment and the resultant depression and stress also make it difficult for women to relax and one midwife felt this could cause problems in later pregnancy if the women were prone to high blood pressure.

Information collected from health records

The examination of health records made it possible to get a more objective view of the effect on pregnant women of living in bed and breakfast hotels.

A mother's age and number of pregnancies are important background factors when looking at a baby's health, since babies born to mothers under 20 or over 35 and those born to women with four or more previous pregnancies are more at risk. Mother's age was not recorded for half the sample in London but in Manchester all the mothers' ages were known. The average age was 21 although one in four was under 20. The greater risk to babies born to such young mothers may, of course, reflect their poorer financial and housing position.

Information on previous pregnancies was better recorded than age. In Manchester the average number of previous pregnancies was 1.4, but four women had four or more previous pregnancies recorded. In London, however, the picture is more complicated.

The mothers of babies born and bred in bed and breakfast had more previous pregnancies, with 18 out of the 41 mothers having had at least four previous pregnancies. A similar pattern was found in the ethnically matched Tower Hamlets sample, where 12 of the 41 mothers had also had four or more previous pregnancies. This reflects to some extent the family structure of the predominantly Asian population.[1]

These findings suggest that some of the women living in bed and breakfast in Manchester and London were those whose babies would have a higher than average risk of being small or sick at birth. They needed extra support and help to ensure that they could eat well during pregnancy, avoid stress and worry and protect their babies from infections and other hazards. Instead they were living in accommodation which increases the risk to themselves and their children.

In Manchester, access to obstetric records provided details of problems recorded in pregnancy and labour. These appear in Table 4.1.

Table 4.1: NUMBER OF WOMEN WITH PROBLEMS RECORDED IN PREGNANCY AND LABOUR (MANCHESTER SAMPLE ONLY)

Problems recorded	Homeless during pregnancy	Homeless after birth
Hospital admission(s)	6	2
Bleeding in pregnancy	4	3
Anaemia	4	1
Foetal distress in labour	2	3
Postpartum haemorrhage	3	2
Weight loss/failure to grow	2	2
Caesarean section	3	1
Infection	3	—
Premature labour	1	—
Anorexia	—	1
Total number with problems recorded	13	5
Average number of problems per woman	2.2	3
Number with no problems recorded	8	16

Note: For comparative purposes, the Manchester sample is divided into two groups, 21 mothers who were in bed and breakfast during the pregnancy and 21 who only moved into bed and breakfast after the birth. These groups correspond roughly with the "born and bred" and "moved in" samples in London.

There is a striking difference between the histories of the women who were in bed and breakfast during pregnancy and those who moved into bed and breakfast after the birth of a baby. Those who were homeless in pregnancy were more than twice as likely to have problems recorded and were three times as likely to have been admitted to hospital during the pregnancy. The incidence of anaemia amongst pregnant women in hotels may reflect the difficulties women face in eating a healthy diet in bed and breakfast hotels. The greater susceptibility of pregnant women to infections could reflect both their generally poor state of health and the epidemics of minor infections endemic to bed and breakfast living, reported by both homeless families and health professionals. Since many homeless families come into bed and breakfast hotels from shared, impermanent or overcrowded housing, often living for short periods with a series of friends and family members, the difference between the sub-sample, who were homeless during pregnancy, and those who became homeless after the birth of their baby is an even more damning indictment of the effects on women's health of living in bed and breakfast.

REFERENCES

1 "Birth Statistics", England and Wales, OPCS. 1986

CHAPTER 5
Food and diet

Introduction and summary

"There's not enough money to buy food for the week and I can't do what I want to do. I feel hungry at night and the kitchen closes at eight thirty. I can get the food if I ask but why should I ask to get my own food? If I was working I'd have to rush home to cook a meal before the kitchen closed."

THE IMPORTANCE of nutrition to long-term and short-term health has been well known for a long time. Current dietary advice is that people should eat plenty of fruit and vegetables, plenty of high-fibre cereal and starchy food, some lean meat, fish, pulses and eggs and a selection of dairy foods. People are in general advised to be careful about the amount of fatty and sugary foods they eat and to ensure that they are getting a variety of food. A healthy balanced diet will provide enough vitamins, minerals and protein for good health and growth and also help protect against other health problems in the future, such as obesity, dental caries, heart disease, high blood pressure, diseases of the large bowel, and some cancers.

As part of the interviews the women were asked what they had had to eat and drink the day before. If this was not typical of their diet they were asked what was; if eating was different at the weekend this was also discussed. To assess the quality of the women's diets they were asked how many times a week they ate 30 different designated foods, and the types of food and meals they ate. They were asked how often they ate fruit, and how often they ate vegetables and salads. The women were also asked about cooking and food storage facilities, how much they spent on food, and how they felt about their diets.

Twenty out of the 48 women in the survey whose diets were analysed were eating a poor diet. There was a heavy reliance on take-aways, cafes and snacks, and on pre-packaged convenience foods. Well over half never had a hotel breakfast. The consumption of fruit and vegetables was generally lower than for other low-income groups in the general population.

The overall quality of the women's diets was affected to a great extent by the availability and cleanliness of a kitchen, storage and food preparation facilities (see Chapter 2). Those with access to a decent kitchen or who had kitchen facilities in their rooms were much more likely to be eating a better diet than those without.

The lack of money was also an important restriction on diet. Nearly a quarter of the women were going without food from time to time because they could not afford it and one in ten said their children sometimes went without food. Money constraints played an even greater part in poor diets in this study than in a comparable study of people with low incomes in the general population, suggesting that living in a bed and breakfast hotel accentuates financial problems.

This study also found that the older women tended to have better diets than the younger ones in the survey. In general those from ethnic minorities managed to prepare meals more often and relied less on snacks compared with the other women in the survey.

The women expressed grave concerns about the poor quality of their diets and the expense. The level of worry was closely related to the women's ability to cater for themselves. Forty-six out of the 57 women in the survey felt that since living in a hotel

> they were eating less well than before. Health visitors were also worried about the diets of families living in hotels and some even expressed fears of malnutrition in children.

The women's diets

"Over Christmas we didn't have anything to eat. I think I'm starving myself."

OF THE 48 women in the survey giving sufficient information for an assessment, only four had "good" diets, 24 had "average" diets and 20 had "poor" diets. (See Note 1 below on the assessment of diets.) Well over a third had diets which were very high in fat and sugar and low in dietary fibre.

Looking at daily meal patterns, seven of the women were living primarily on "snacks" only occasionally supplemented with a hot meal, 22 were eating one or two "meals" plus "snacks", while the remaining 19 were eating three "meals" a day. (See Note 2 below on the definition of a "meal" and a "snack".)

In spite of hotel accommodation being generally referred to as "bed and breakfast", well over half the women never had a hotel breakfast. This was either because none was provided or there were other problems such as the times at which it was available, or as one woman put it, "it's inedible". The others did have a hotel breakfast most days or every day, and two families sometimes had other hotel meals which they paid for separately.

Looking at the types of food the 48 women ate most, 14 lived mainly on "convenience" food, 14 got most of their meals from cafes or take-aways, while 20 were eating mainly fresh food. (See Note 3 below on the definition of "fresh" and "convenience" foods.)

Reflecting the problems of storing, preparing and cooking food, over a third of the women never prepared a cooked meal for their families, or did so less than once a week. Only just over a quarter prepared cooked meals more than once a day. Otherwise the women relied on take-aways and cafes; one in four said they had take-aways at least four times a week, while cafes were frequented less often. Some depended on getting cooked meals elsewhere such as with friends or relatives.

> "Eating junk food makes you feel weak. I feel I'm going to collapse. If I don't go to my sister's I don't get a staple meal all week."

All current dietary advice stresses the importance of fruit and vegetables for contributing towards the vitamin, mineral and fibre content of the diet.[1] The amount of fruit and vegetables eaten by the women in this survey was generally low, with about half eating fruit and/or vegetables and salad three times a week or less. Nine were eating these foods less than once a week while two women virtually never ate fruit, vegetables or salad.

Table 5.1: CONSUMPTION OF FRUIT AND VEGETABLES COMPARED WITH INTAKES IN THE NORTH OF ENGLAND IN 1984

Types of food	Eating these foods daily			
	Homeless women		North of England	
	number	%	number	%
Vegetables & salad	20	40	319	60
Fruit juice in cartons	17	35	65	12
Total in group	48		530	

The hotel women's consumption of fruit, vegetables and salad found in this survey appears to be lower than that of women from other low-income groups. For example a survey in the north of England in 1984 found that about 60 per cent of the people with low incomes interviewed were eating fresh vegetables daily compared with only 40 per cent in this study (see Table 5.1).[2]

However, many more women in this study were drinking fruit juice in cartons, which may in part reflect a general increase in consumption of these drinks over the last two years.

To illustrate how poor the diets of some of the women in this survey were, Table 5.2. shows what four of them recalled eating the day before the interview: in each case they said these had been fairly typical days.

Factors affecting the women's diets

Facilities for preparing and cooking food.

The availability and cleanliness of the kitchen and food storage and preparation facilities were major factors affecting the overall quality of the women's diets. All four women with a good diet used the kitchen facilities available to them. Over half of the 24 women who did not have kitchen facilities, either because there were none available or because they did not use the kitchen, had poor diets (see Table 5.3).

Having cooking facilities in their own rooms seemed to help the women eat more healthily. Of the four with good diets, one had no facilities in her room but the other three had rings, a grill and an oven. Seven of the 24 women with average diets had rings, three had a grill, and three had an oven. Of the 20 women with poor diets, only two had rings, one had a grill and one had an oven.

A number of women who did not use the kitchen in the premises prepared their meals elsewhere. It was clear that those who cooked their own meals, whether in the hotel, at the home of relatives or friends, or at a local centre specifically provided for

Table 5.2: ACTUAL CONSUMPTION OF FOOD THE DAY BEFORE THE INTERVIEW

Time of day and type of food that day	Woman 1 (pregnant)	Woman 2	Woman 3	Woman 4
Breakfast	White toast and jam Tea with milk & sugar	White bread and butter Tea with milk & sugar	Sugar puffs and milk	Cornflakes with milk and sugar Fried egg, bacon and sausage Tea with milk
Lunch	Chicken and chips	Chicken and chips	Apple and grapes Fizzy orange	Tea with milk
Afternoon	Tea with milk & sugar	—	Biscuits	—
Tea or later	Fish and chips	Cornflakes and milk	Steamed fish & mashed potato cake	Buttered popcorn
Fruit	Less than once a week	1-3 times a week	4-6 times a week	Never
Vegetables or Salad	Never	Never	Less than once a week	Less than once a week
Cakes, sweets, biscuits and chocolates	Never	Never	Daily	4-6 times a week

NOTE 1: ASSESSMENT OF DIETS

In assessing the overall quality of the diet, it was assumed that a good quality diet would include at least three portions of cereal foods or starchy vegetables each day, at least three portions of fruit, salad or vegetables each day, one or two portions of protein-rich foods which were relatively low in saturated fats (such as lean meat, fish, pulses, beans or nuts), and at least one or two portions of dairy foods such as milk, cheese and yogurt. A "good" diet would include only limited amounts of sweet foods, such as cakes, biscuits, sweets and chocolates. The assessment of overall quality also took account of the women's fat, sugar and fibre intakes. A cross-check was made by doing a nutrient analysis, based on all the available information about food intakes, and using standard U.K. food tables in a computer package.[3] The diets of the women were assessed as "poor", "average" and "good".

NOTE 2: DEFINITION OF "MEAL" AND "SNACK"

A "meal" is defined as a breakfast or a cooked main meal, or a sandwich or salad-type meal, which is eaten at a regular time each day and contains some sort of meat, fish, beans, egg or dairy food and some bread, potatoes, rice, pasta etc. It may or may not include fruit, vegetables or salad. A "snack" is defined as a single food eaten at an irregular time, e.g. biscuits, cakes, sweets, crisps, chips etc.

NOTE 3: DEFINITION OF "FRESH" AND "CONVENIENCE" FOODS

Fresh food includes bread, cheese, milk, fresh and frozen meat, vegetables and fish. Convenience food includes pre-packaged food such as pies, pasties, instant meals in pots and packaged soups and desserts.

Table 5.3: RELATIONSHIP BETWEEN THE QUALITY OF THE WOMEN'S DIETS AND THEIR USE OF KITCHEN FACILITIES

Use of kitchen facilities   Overall quality of diet

Number of women

Use of kitchen facilities	Good	Average	Poor	Total
Yes	4	12	7	23
No	0	4	3	7
None available	0	7	10	17
Not known	0	1	0	1
Total	4	24	20	48

homeless families (such as the Bayswater Project Playgroup in London) tended to eat more fresh than convenience foods (see Table 5.4). For example, of the four women preparing almost all their own meals, three ate mainly fresh food. Fifteen women were preparing fewer than three meals a week and of them only four were eating mainly fresh food.

Table 5.4: RELATIONSHIP BETWEEN TYPES OF FOOD AND THE NUMBER OF MEALS THE WOMEN COOKED EACH WEEK.

Number of own meals cooked per week	Mainly fresh food	Mainly convenience food	Mainly take-away & cafe food	Total
Less than 1	4	3	8	15
1-3	0	2	2	4
4-7	6	5	4	15
8-14	7	3	0	10
More than 15	3	1	0	4
Total	20	14	14	48

The amount of vegetables and salad eaten was also affected by whether or not kitchen facilities were available. Nearly all the women using a kitchen ate vegetables and salad more than four times a week, half of them doing so daily. A third of the women who did not use a kitchen hardly ever ate vegetables or salad.

However problems arose with the large number of people sharing kitchens. This meant that people could not eat when they wanted to or when the children were hungry, and once in the kitchen they felt pressurised to cook only quick meals as others were waiting.

> **"When I'm hungry, someone else is using the cooker. Your timing goes up the creek. If I had my own cooker I could eat regularly."**

One woman whose kitchen facilities were in the basement more than two floors away said: "I don't like sitting in the kitchen to eat because people come in and out all the time, so I have to carry the food upstairs and it gets cold."

The place where they could prepare their food seemed to influence the quality of the women's diets. Over three quarters of those with poor diets were unhappy in some way about the food preparation area. This was a considerably higher proportion than amongst the other women.

The cleanliness of the hotel in general and of the kitchen in particular were also important factors. Whilst 33 of the 48 women did not feel there were problems with the overall cleanliness of the hotel, 15 did — six of whom reported dirty kitchens and ten of whom reported concern about bugs. Of these 15 women, one had a good diet, five had an average diet, and nine had a poor diet.

Money

When asked if they had to go without food for themselves because they couldn't afford it, nearly a quarter of the women said they did from time to time and ten per cent said that occasionally their children had to go without food as well. Of the 12 women who went without food, nine had poor diets.

> **"Sometimes I run out of food and money and I have to go without for a couple of days."**

A previous study of people in the north of England with low incomes, which included pensioners but not the homeless, found that 11 per cent of the people asked did not have enough money for food all week.[4] Compared to the figure of nearly 25 per cent going without food in this survey, this suggests that the extra burden of homelessness may make it even more difficult to find the money to pay for food. This would be in keeping with a study of homeless people in the London Borough of Camden in 1985 which found that residents in many of the 14 hotels where rents were very high had to subsidise their bed and breakfast payments with their entire food allowance.[5]

Lack of money for food seemed to have an adverse effect on the women's meal patterns, the types of food they were eating, and the frequency with which they ate vegetables and salad. Over half of the women eating mainly snacks were cutting back on food because they couldn't afford to eat better whereas only one in ten of those eating three meals a day was cutting back for this reason. None of the 20 women eating mainly fresh foods felt they ever had to go without their own food. However over a third of those eating convenience foods and half those eating mainly from take-aways and cafes did feel they sometimes had to go without.

Women who did not feel they had to go without anything for financial reasons ate vegetables and salads more often than the others. Three-quarters of them ate vegetables and salads frequently whilst nearly half the women who went without food from time to time, hardly ever did.

Age

In general, the older women tended to have better diets than the younger women, as illustrated in Table 5.5.

Meal patterns also appeared to be affected by the women's age. The women over 25 ate more regular meals and depended less on snacks. Half the women over 25 ate regularly whilst only one fifth of the women under 25 did.

Table 5.5: RELATIONSHIP BETWEEN THE QUALITY OF THE WOMEN'S DIETS AND THE AGES OF THE WOMEN

Age of women

Overall quality of the diet

Number of women

	Good	Average	Poor	Total
Under 20 years	0	2	2	4
20-24 years	0	6	9	15
25-29 years	2	9	5	16
Over 30 years	2	5	3	10
Not known	0	2	1	3
Total	4	24	20	48

Ethnic origin

As numbers were small, it was difficult to assess the impact of ethnic origin on the quality of the women's diets. However, the Asian women in the sample appeared to have much more regular eating habits than any other group, a factor which in itself often points to a better diet (see Tables 5.6 and 5.7).

Table 5.6: MEAL PATTERNS RELATED TO ETHNIC ORIGIN

Ethnic origin

Meal patterns

Number of women

	3 meals	1-2 meals + snacks	Snacks	Total
Afro-Caribbean	0	4	2	6
African	0	2	0	2
Asian	7	0	1	8
Vietnamese	1	1	0	2
Irish	3	3	0	6
Other white	7	10	4	21
Other	1	2	0	3
Total	19	22	7	48

At least half of the African, Asian, Vietnamese and Irish women were eating mainly fresh food, but this was not true of the other groups. The highest proportion of women eating take-away and cafe food was in the "other white" group. From the small figures, it appears that those from ethnic minorities (who tend to eat very differently from white British women) make great efforts to carry on eating the same sort of fresh foods as they have done previously.

One GP who was working with a number of Bangladeshi families suggested that their diet was responsible for undernourishment. However the health visitors and midwives who visit Bangladeshi families strongly disagreed. They felt that the families coped remarkably well given the lack of facilities and their diet would probably be adequate if they had access to reasonable facilities.

Meal patterns

Whilst regular meal patterns do not guarantee a good quality diet, they make a considerable impact. Over half of the women having three meals regularly each day were eating mainly fresh food. None of the seven women living on snacks was, nor did they have good or even average quality diets.

Table 5.7: THE RELATIONSHIP BETWEEN MEAL PATTERNS AND OVERALL QUALITY OF WOMEN'S DIETS

Overall quality of the diet	Meal Patterns — Number of women			
	3 meals	1-2 meals + snacks	Snacks	Total
Good	2	2	0	4
Average	13	11	0	24
Poor	4	9	7	20
Total	19	22	7	48

From the study it was found that the homeless women with regular meal patterns ate vegetables and salads considerably more often than those eating mainly snacks. While over half the women eating three meals a day ate vegetables and salads daily, none of those eating mainly snacks did. Over half the women living on snacks ate vegetables and salads less than once a week.

The women's feelings about their diets

"I'm worried about where the next meal will come from. It's mainly junk food. It's not good especially when I'm pregnant."

All the women were asked how they felt about their diet and whether they were happy with it. Only ten of the 57 women felt they had no problems. For the remainder the most pressing problem was the expense, followed by an awareness that their diets were not good for their health (see Table 5.8).

Table 5.8: THE WOMEN'S FEELINGS ABOUT THEIR DIET

Feelings about diet	Number of women stating problem
No problem	10
Expensive	27
Bad for health	25
Boring and limited	21
No choice	20
Often feel hungry	12
Nowhere to sit and eat	9
Other	13
No answer	3
Total women in survey	57

Many also said their diet was boring or limited and they had little choice of food. Comments were often made about their reliance on "junk food" and lack of vegetables, and 12 women said they often felt hungry. One woman was particularly concerned because she had a stomach ulcer, yet had to rely heavily on take-aways. As she said; "it's grease or grease".

Table 5.9: PROBLEMS CONNECTED WITH FOOD AND EATING EXPERIENCED BY WOMEN WITH GOOD, POOR AND AVERAGE DIETS

Number of women mentioning each problem

Good diet		Average diet		Poor diet	
No problems	3	No problems	7	No problems	0
Bad for health	1	Expensive	8	Bad for health	11
Lack of choice	1	Boring/limited	6	Expensive	10
Other	1	Bad for health	6	Boring/limited	10
		Lack of choice	6	Lack of choice	8
		Nowhere to eat	5	Often hungry	7
		Often hungry	3	Nowhere to eat	4
		Other	4	Other	8
		No answer	3		
Total number	4	Total number	24	Total number	20

The type of food the women ate affected how they felt about their food. Not surprisingly all the women who were eating mainly take-away and cafe food were unhappy with their diets. Just under half the women eating fresh foods and over three-quarters of those eating convenience foods were also unhappy. Of the four with good quality diets, three felt that they had no problems. The people who were eating more convenience and take-away foods were also less happy about the way they were feeding their children than those who were eating predominantly fresh foods.

Worries and difficulties about food and eating seemed to be closely tied up with the availability of acceptable cooking facilities in the hotel. Those women who were able to go somewhere else for meals, such as to friends, relatives or a local centre, were much happier about food and eating generally.

None of the women felt they were eating better now than they had before moving to a hotel: altogether, 46 out of the 57 women said they were eating less well. As one put it, "having a decent meal is a luxury".

Comments from health professionals

All the health visitors contacted were concerned about the diets of families living in hotels. A health visitor in London summarised the dietary problems faced by homeless families. "On the whole, families in hotels fully understand what food they should be eating, but it falls apart when you have to live in a hotel room. Even if there are cooking facilities in the hotel, invariably there are too many families sharing, and people have to prepare food in rooms. Imagine what it's like with a toddler wanting to eat — you end up giving it crisps and things like that to keep it quiet. It's the same for mothers. They are stressed and cannot prepare a decent meal for themselves, so they live on buns and cups of coffee because those kind of things can be prepared in a room."

The story was similar in Southend and Manchester, where one health visitor felt that the diet "almost amounts to malnutrition standards in some cases". Health visitors also see overweight homeless children whose problems are caused by an imbalanced diet and excessive amounts of unsuitable foods such as chips.

In a Health Visitors Association/Shelter survey two-thirds of the health visitors responding to the questionnaire confirmed that they were concerned about malnutrition.[6] Health visitors throughout the country indicated that the absence of adequate cooking facilities and refrigeration in most of the hotels meant many families were relying on take-away meals, supplemented by illicitly-cooked food. Many families had to leave hotel rooms between 10am and 4pm and this also affected their eating habits and nutritional intake.

REFERENCES

1   "Eating for health", DHSS, HMSO. 1978.
"Nutritional Guidelines for Health Education in Britain. A report of the National Advisory Committee on Nutrition Education". Health Education Council. 1983.
"Diet and Cardiovascular disease". *Reports on Health and Social Subjects, No. 28.* DHSS. 1984.
"Household food consumption and expenditure", *1986 Annual Report of the National Food Survey Committee,* MAFF, HMSO. 1987.
Isobel Cole-Hamilton and Tim Lang, *Tightening belts: a report on the impact of poverty on food,* The London Food Commission. June 1986.
2   Tim Lang et al, *Jam Tomorrow?,* Food Policy Unit, Manchester Polytechnic. 1984.
3   A. Paul and D. Southgate, *McCance and Widdowson's: The composition of foods,* 4th edition, HMSO. 1978.
4   Tim Lang et al, *op.cit.*
5   "Board and lodging: effect of new regulations on non-priority homeless claimants". Report of the Director of Housing, London Borough of Camden. 1985.
6   "Health visitors and homeless families", *Health Visitors Journal,* November 1986.
Jonathan Stearn, "An expensive way of making children ill", *Roof* Magazine. September/October 1986.

Unemployed family doing their shopping. London 1986.

CHAPTER **6**

Children's health and diet

Introduction and summary

BABIES IN HOTELS have a poorer start to life than most. The findings of this study suggest that babies born to mothers living in hotels tend to have a low birthweight. Health professionals, aware of the poor conditions in many hotels, often try to keep newborn babies in hospital longer when the mother lives in a hotel. Nevertheless the mother must eventually cope with the physical and mental stresses of having a tiny baby in a hotel room: these problems are highlighted in this study.

All young children in hotels tend to suffer frequently from a range of illnesses. This may be partly a result of the unhygienic conditions in many hotels but is also likely to result from the stresses that the children feel. The survey found that children are often confined to hotel rooms for long periods of time and young children may be very physically restricted to keep them from danger. Both the mothers and the health professionals identified behaviour problems and slow development in hotel children. They are also more likely to suffer accidents caused by the dangerous environment they have to live in which is not suitable for safe healthy family life.

Because of the lack of adequate facilities for preparing meals, mothers were especially concerned about their children's diet. However the poor diet of the mothers often forces them to give up breastfeeding and rely on bottles for young babies which, in a hotel, carries a grave risk of infection.

In spite of being a high risk group, hotel children seem to have poor access to health services. Records suggest that they tend to miss developmental checks, immunisations and vaccinations.

Newborn babies in hotels

Birthweight

BIRTHWEIGHT IS PROBABLY the single most important indicator of a baby's future health. Small, frail babies are less likely to survive pregnancy, more likely to suffer congenital handicaps, more susceptible to life-threatening infections and less likely to enjoy a healthy childhood.

Analysis of the health records shows that, although the number of cases is small, the proportion of small babies born to homeless families in London does give cause for concern with about a quarter of the children born in bed and breakfast hotels having a low birthweight (see Table 6.1).

This is considerably higher than the national average of seven per cent of babies born with a low birthweight. The born and bred sample includes a high proportion of families with Bangladeshi, Indian and Pakistani surnames: nationally 11 per cent of babies born to mothers who come from Bangladesh or India are low birthweight, as are 18 per cent of those born to mothers from Pakistan. Therefore ethnic origin does not wholly account for the very high numbers of small babies amongst the hotel homeless and this suggests that living in bed and breakfast accommodation itself may be an important factor. (The Tower Hamlets control group includes an even higher proportion of Asian families than the hotel born and bred sample, yet it had a much lower incidence of low birthweight.)

Table 6.1: BIRTHWEIGHT IN THE RECORDS ANALYSIS

	London samples*				Manchester sample**
	Born & bred	Moved in	Hackney	Tower Hamlets	
−2500gms	10(25%)	5(10%)	4(10%)	6(15%)	5(12.5%)
2500+gms	31	44	37	35	27
Not known	—	—	—	—	8

*Born & bred — born and still living in hotels. Moved in — moved into hotels after the birth. Hackney — control sample matches for age and sex with born and bred sample, drawn from same clinic. Tower Hamlets control sample matched for age and sex with born and bred sample, drawn from a Tower Hamlets clinic.

**Excludes one set of twins who were low birthweight;

Mothers' and health professionals' concerns about newborn babies

Five out of the 19 babies in this survey born while their mothers were living in a hotel were premature, including two with a low birthweight. One mother attributed her baby's small size and need for an incubator to her poor diet during pregnancy. Altogether five of these 19 babies had not been healthy at birth and two had stayed in hospital for over ten days. The mothers were very worried about their newborn babies and felt that hotel life was bad for them.

Health professionals were equally concerned. After birth, babies are most vulnerable for the first seven days of life and in all three areas the midwives agreed that women in bed and breakfast hotels were often encouraged to stay in hospital longer than normal after giving birth, because of the poor conditions they would be returning to. In Southend the midwife estimated that 50 per cent of women are asked to stay in longer and they could be kept in hospital up to ten days after giving birth. Mothers as well as newborn babies can benefit from this. One midwife explained that "this gives the women a chance to rest and recuperate, plus cuts down the risk of infection to the mother".

In Manchester, it is standard practice to write to hospitals when a woman is in a hotel requesting that she is not discharged before five days. In London, midwives suggested that at least 60 per cent of mothers from hotels are asked to stay the maximum of five days before going back to their hotel rooms.

"It is virtually impossible for a mother with a new baby to cope when she is at the top of the hotel and the kitchen is down in the basement."

All the midwives expressed concern about the effects of the

introduction of a new baby into an already overcrowded hotel room. The unsuitable surroundings naturally worried mothers and disruption to older children tended to increase family tensions.

The GP in Hounslow was particularly concerned for women who have been placed in a hotel far from their own community and support network. His patients included a large number of homeless Bangladeshi women. With language forming a potential barrier and their reluctance to be in the care of a male doctor, it is likely that these women in particular would not get adequate treatment for themselves and their newborn babies.

Babies' and children's illnesses

"My daughter was ill with one thing after another from October to March. In summer we can spend more time outside, but I'm dreading this winter."

There were 71 children under five years old in the interview sample of homeless women, as well as 39 older children. Nearly half of the children under five had suffered from diarrhoea, mostly with sickness, since living in a hotel, and over a third had been getting chest infections — a higher incidence than would normally be expected. Infections seemed to be passed quickly from one child to another and 18 women said that coughs and colds were almost constant amongst the children. Five mothers mentioned that their children had developed skin problems since living in a hotel. Several women felt that the children's health problems resulted from their poor diet in the hotel. Of the under-fives who had previously lived elsewhere over two-thirds were felt to have generally worse health since moving to a hotel.

"She was never ill before we came here, but now she's ill all the time. Before she was growing nicely but now she's not getting good food and doesn't eat properly."

The health professionals were convinced that poor hygiene, overcrowding, shared washing facilities and the lack of amenities in hotels all contribute to the spread of infectious diseases. In one hotel in Finsbury Park, London, there have been nearly 30 cases of chickenpox and a serious outbreak of hepatitis B.[1]

"It's very difficult to keep things clean and sterile when you are washing and preparing food in the same sink that you have just washed a baby's nappy in."

In one hotel a woman reported that there was no kitchen for the hotel residents to use and kettles were not allowed in the bedrooms. Although the rules forbade food in the rooms, she kept cereal for her baby and mixed the powdered milk with hot water from the tap with a high risk of infection to the child.

As one health visitor in Southend pointed out, "If the families were not living in hotels, they would keep children in if they were ill. Instead they live cheek-by-jowl with other families, and have to take their children out for take-aways. It's not surprising that things like whooping cough, German measles and chickenpox spread like wildfire around the hotels." Minor accidents were also common and one doctor claimed to see at least one burn on a homeless child every week because families have to use kettles in the bedroom. Several health professionals felt that living in a hotel room is not conducive to normal child health and development.

The children's behaviour and development

The survey found that many of the children seemed to react strongly to their immediate environment and behaved, ate and slept better when out of the hotel: one would scream when he was brought back to the room; three children aged four and five years had become regular bed-wetters (in one case the child shared a bed with her mother). Several mothers felt their children's development had been affected, and they were slow for their age. Altogether over two-thirds of the mothers felt their children had been affected in some way by moving into a hotel.

> "My little girl is very aggressive and unhappy. She wants to go out and gets frustrated because there's nowhere here to play. She becomes very agitated and often won't eat for days."

Over half the children were felt by their mothers to have become very bad sleepers for their age; over a third were felt to have developed major eating problems, and nearly a quarter were identified as being unusually aggressive or active. Many mothers felt their children's behaviour had deteriorated and they had become "wild", "cheeky" or "out of control". Others had become withdrawn, miserable, bored, restless or unsettled; several mentioned regular nightmares.

> "They seem very tense and aware of the situation, leading to naughtiness, tantrums and screaming. I can't tell them to go to another room. You just have to put up with it somehow."

Health professionals shared this concern for the children's behaviour and development. Those included in this study saw a direct link between the slow development of children and the accommodation that the families live in, rather than inherent problems with the families. Because of all the dangers in hotels, some mothers are forced to leave their babies in cots or strap their young children into high-chairs or push-chairs for long periods of time. One health visitor felt that many children cling to their cots because of the insecurity caused by moving from one hotel to another.

One of the health visitors in Manchester had moved from being a generic health visitor to seeing only hotel families. As she pointed out, "I have seen families before they became homeless, and it is very easy to see the behavioural changes that occur as soon as they move into hotel rooms — even though they may not have been living in ideal conditions before."

> "Hotel children are often later walkers, late talkers and slow in keeping themselves clean. You often see children still walking around in nappies at three years old."

A paediatrician who sees a large number of hotel children in London went so far as to link speech delays to the lack of play experience. "When children begin to get mobile they develop their motor skills. Lack of play opportunities, plus a depressed mother, lead to an understimulated child who is slow to develop." Research in Bayswater, London, found that up to a third of children in hotels had possible behavioural problems.[2] Joint research by the Health Visitors Association and Shelter found that nearly all the health visitors who responded mentioned emotional and behavioural problems as one of their key concerns.[3] The mothers in this survey were very anxious about their children's health and behaviour but felt there was little they could do about it. This in turn, accentuated the mothers' own stress.

Accidents

During the interviews it emerged that 22 children had had some kind of accident. These included falling downstairs while playing; knocking into furniture or falling in the cramped bedrooms; and hurting themselves on the fire doors in the corridors. One child had fallen through a gap in the stair banisters. The inadequate storage for all the family's possessions in the bedroom had also caused some accidents as children had managed to get hold of dangerous articles including caustic soda, disinfectant and razor blades. Other common accidents are burns from kettles, gas rings and unguarded heaters, injuries from falling out of bed because there are no cots and children falling downstairs because there is nowhere else to play.

The mothers expressed a fear of accidents in hotels which is not unfounded. All the health visitors interviewed also remarked on the danger to small children from being cramped into premises that are grossly unsuitable for family life, with no safe play area.

"Once you have introduced a kettle, that is definitely a hazard and the number of scalds we see appears to be higher than in other families."

One health visitor described how a one-year-old received third degree burns from her hip to her ankle when her mother spilt a pot of hot water over her, while carrying the child and the pot up from the basement kitchen to the bedroom. Even fire doors themselves can be a hazard: in Bayswater a child managed to get out of the fire door and then fell through the roof outside.

Play facilities for children

Mothers in hotel rooms are faced with the impossible choice of allowing their children to play in the dangerous environment of the hotel, or stopping them from playing and thus restricting their development.

Children's play is often seen as a major problem for homeless families living in hotels, and the interview survey confirmed this. Well over a third of the under-fives normally spent eight or more hours in the bedroom during the day and almost as many normally spent five to eight hours in the room during the day. The main worries the mothers expressed about play were the lack of space and fears about safety, especially where the children had to play on the stairs or in the hall as an alternative to being confined in a bedroom; they were also concerned that they could run out into the street. Those who were able to take the children to a playgroup were very appreciative of the access to toys and space it provided. Many would have liked there to be a well-equipped common room for play in the hotel itself. None of the hotels in the survey had this provision, in spite of the fact that most seemed to be used exclusively for homeless families.

The children's food and diet

Mothers were very concerned about their children's diet. When asked if they were satisfied with the way in which they could feed their children, the vast majority said they were not, and there was most dissatisfaction amongst the women with children who lived mainly on snack foods or who had a poor quality diet.

The women with babies under two were asked whether or not they had any problems with preparing food for them. More than half of the 34 mothers this applied to said they did, particularly with warming food and storage. In general, midwives still try to encourage homeless mothers to breastfeed rather than bottle-feed. As a Manchester midwife explained, "Bottle feeding has a high risk of gastro-enteritis. A mother can sterilise the bottle and then put it down for a minute in the lounge. Another child may touch the bottle teat, and infect it, and the mother gives it to her baby without noticing. That would not happen if she were living in a flat on her own."

Powdered baby milk has to be prepared with previously boiled water. Yet because of fire and safety restrictions, some hotels do not let mothers have kettles in their rooms. In Manchester, mothers in one hotel had to ask the receptionist to get hot water from a geyser without any certainty that it had actually been boiled. One father, who was refused hot water in the hotel, had to go down the street to the local newsagent and ask them to boil a kettle to make a baby's feed. As the midwife pointed out, "That was a well-motivated family. I would imagine the average mother may not be bothered to go to such extremes and be tempted to use the hot tap to feed a baby that is screaming."

In spite of the high risk of infection involved in bottle feeding babies in hotels, one midwife estimated that 50 per cent of the mothers she visited in hotels were forced to give up breastfeeding within two weeks because a poor diet prevented them from producing enough milk.

Health records of the children's development

In order that any delay in development or any handicap can be quickly picked up and treated, child health clinics regularly assess children's physical and social development, their hearing, vision and use of language. Children are usually tested at six weeks, six to eight months and 12 to 15 months. Homeless children's health records were examined to see whether these regular assessments were carried out, as shown in Table 6.2.

Assessments seem to be the most efficiently recorded for young children in London, but the very high proportion of "moved in" babies who had no check at six weeks is particularly worrying since this is a crucial early assessment when physical problems can be discovered which may be treated at an early stage. In Manchester, there was less variation in the recording of assessments at the different ages, but again the low level of take-up of the first critical examination must give rise to special concern.

Table 6.2: CHILDREN WITH NO HEALTH ASSESSMENT
(Percentages of those who had reached the appropriate age)

Age of Child	London samples				Manchester sample**
	Born & bred	Moved in	Hackney	Tower Hamlets	
6 weeks	12%(^{5}/41)	51%(^{25}/49)	12%(^{5}/41)	10%(^{4}/41)	42%(^{10}/24)
6-8 months	68%(^{23}/34)	78%(^{35}/45)	49%(^{17}/35)	80%(^{28}/35)*	41%(^{9}/22)
12-15 months	74%(^{14}/19)	75%(^{24}/32)	65%(^{11}/17)	4%(^{1}/24)	27%(^{4}/15)

*In Tower Hamlets the assessment was not routinely carried out at six months.

**The table shows information for physical examinations at each age for the London children. For Manchester it shows whether any information about developmental assessment was recorded.

The sample for Manchester is smaller than the sample used in Table 6.1 because a smaller number of infant records were available.

Immunisation and vaccination

Another key role for the health services is to give immunisations and vaccinations at particular ages as part of the baby clinic routine. The extent to which children's immunisations are up-to-date while they are in bed and breakfast accommodation is shown in Table 6.3. For the samples of children in London still living in bed and breakfast, the information applies to January 1987; in Manchester it applies to the date of rehousing.

In general more children in bed and breakfast hotels missed immunisations. In Manchester the numbers are higher than for the authority as a whole, and in London the control groups generally fare much better than those in bed and breakfast. The somewhat better record for children born and bred in hotels who do better on all immunisations except measles may indicate that Hackney's special mobile clinic for homeless families has improved access to and use of services.

Table 6.3: CHILDREN WITH NO IMMUNISATION OR VACCINATIONS

(Numbers and as percentages of those who had reached the appropriate age)

	London sample			Manchester*		
Type of immunisation**	Born & bred	Moved In	Hackney	Tower Hamlets	Bed & Breakfast sample	Local pop
BCG	19%($^8/_{41}$)	26%($^{13}/_{49}$)	22%($^9/_{41}$)	15%($^6/_{41}$)	73%($^{16}/_{22}$)	—
DT/DPT	32%($^{11}/_{34}$)	40%($^{17}/_{42}$)	29%($^{10}/_{34}$)	15%($^5/_{34}$)	50%($^{11}/_{22}$)	20%
Polio	32%($^{11}/_{34}$)	40%($^{17}/_{42}$)	29%($^{10}/_{34}$)	12%($^4/_{34}$)	50%($^{11}/_{22}$)	20%
Measles	69%($^9/_{13}$)	48%($^{10}/_{21}$)	31%($^4/_{13}$)	31%($^4/_{13}$)	67%($^8/_{12}$)	52%

* It was possible to compare the bed and breakfast sample with the general population in South Manchester of babies born in 1983.
**BCG immunisations (against TB) are usually given at six weeks; diphtheria and tetanus (DT), or diphtheria, whooping cough and tetanus (DPT), commonly known as the triple, are given at about three, five and nine months. Polio immunisation is given orally at the same times. Measles is given at about 14 months and fewer of the children in the study were old enough to have this vaccination. BCGs were offered routinely by the London health authorities in the study, but in Manchester the maternity hospital where most of the homeless babies were born had only recently begun to offer BCG routinely after the children in this study were born.

These findings are confirmed by another study in Hackney where a sample of over 400 homeless children from hotels just starting school found that nearly half were not immunised at all.[4] The spread of infectious diseases was a major concern for health workers in Manchester and Southend. One paediatrician expressed her concern about the large number of children in hotels who are not immunised. "You feel that if there was an outbreak of polio or diphtheria it would whistle through the hotels." In spite of being a high risk group, children and babies living in hotels seem to have poor access to child health services.

REFERENCES

1. Jonathan Stearn, "An expensive way of making children ill." *Roof* Magazine. September/October 1986.
2. T.D. Wilson, "Health Research among the Homeless", Master of Science dissertation for the London School of Hygiene and Tropical Medicine. September 1986
3. Jonathan Stearn, *op. cit.*
   "Health visitors and homeless families," *Health Visitors Journal,* November 1986.
4. Study by City and Hackney District Health Authority. October 1984.

CHAPTER 7
Health care

Introduction and summary

GIVEN THE HIGH incidence of illness, accidents and stress experienced by those who live in hotels, easy access to health services is particularly important. However, this survey shows that many hotel residents have difficulty getting primary health care and few are getting the extra level of support which may be needed.

In all three areas in this study, it was alleged that hotel families have difficulties registering with GPs. However some attempts are now being made by the health services to ensure homeless families can register. Health visitors and midwives often feel that they are unable to provide an adequate level of service because their caseloads are so large and they

> often do not receive adequate information about homeless families placed in hotels in their area.
> There have been several initiatives to improve health care for homeless people. However it is sometimes argued that if separate specialist services are provided for the homeless, the main health services may then tend to ignore their needs and they may end up with a second-class service.
> This study suggests that the health services need to make far more serious attempts to meet the needs of families in hotels, who are amongst the most vulnerable in society.

The women's perceptions of available health care

"They could push more on our behalf. Why don't they protest? They know how bad the conditions are."

THE WOMEN interviewed were asked a number of questions about their access to health services and any problems they had experienced. Of the 57 women, 23 were still going to the doctor they had prior to moving to a hotel, 13 had permanently registered with a doctor in the area of the hotel and 19 were temporarily registered locally; two had no GP at all. (Temporary registration means that medical records are not transferred.) Half the children under five in the survey were only temporarily registered with a local doctor, just over a quarter were permanently registered locally and the rest were still with the doctor in their previous area.

In spite of the fact that people in London are much more likely to have been placed in a hotel some considerable distance from where they had been living before, the women here were far more likely to be using their previous GP than those in Manchester and Southend, with fewer having permanent or temporary registration with a more local doctor.

Some did not wish to change doctors until finally rehoused, but 14 of the 39 women in London had tried to register with a GP nearer the hotel and had found difficulty in doing so; three of the 18 women in Manchester and Southend also had problems in registering with a local doctor. Many felt that doctors did not want to accept homeless hotel residents. In one case a woman had tried five different GPs before finding one who would take her. One GP had refused to register a family until he received a hospital letter which persuaded him to take on the child, but he continued to refuse to register the rest of the family. One woman was particularly worried that she could not find a local doctor because she had a gynaecological problem and wanted to discuss it.

Five of the women in the survey said that if they or their families needed medical treatment they would have to go to a hospital. In fact 20 of the children and four of the mothers had visited a hospital casualty department since living in a hotel.

Altogether 20 out of the 57 women said they were not happy with their access to medical help. Those who were still registered with a doctor in their previous area, or who had no GP, were more likely to find access a problem than those with temporary or permanent registration locally. Eight hotels in the survey did not have a telephone which the residents could use and several mothers were worried that they would not be able to contact a doctor in an emergency at night. One hotel in Manchester had a regular visit from a GP, but he had to use the TV room and consultations took place in front of everyone.

Because of the poor and crowded conditions in most hotels, the need for health visitors to keep a close eye on the health of young children living in hotels is especially acute. Health visitors may be the first to identify a problem and are often the most regular form of access to health services for the whole family. Only 14 of the 46 children under three years old in this study had a health visitor who came to see them regularly: a further 15 saw a health visitor sometimes, seven had had a visit once or rarely, and eight had never had a visit at all. Where the health visitors had been to the hotel, the first visit had generally been within the first month of birth or of moving into the hotel.

"**The doctors don't ask where you are living or what it's like. They don't take much interest.**"

In spite of the problems which some families had with access to health services, nearly half the women felt that since living in a hotel they had more need to use the health services. Of those who could make the comparison, over two-thirds said that their children had also had to make more use of the health services. The two women who said they used the health services less often than before said this was because their GP was a long way away from where they now lived, not because their need was necessarily less.

Problems with primary health care: GP's

Registering with a GP

Access to primary health care is essential and general practitioners are the gatekeepers of the National Health Service. Homeless people are faced with many health problems particular to hotel life, yet in Southend, Manchester and London health workers reported that homeless families face real difficulties registering with

GPs. One health visitor in London believed that families often had to go to hospital instead of a GP to receive treatment.

"Often I can only get GPs to accept homeless families when I can convince the doctor that the family is of good character and has fallen on hard times."

Several health professionals in this study felt there was a lack of concern shown by some GPs. One health visitor explained that when they discover that a potential patient lives in a hotel, GPs sometimes say that their books are full. The problem has been recognised in Bayswater where the Family Practitioner Committee (FPC) has drawn up a list of GPs who say they are willing to take homeless families. If the family is refused by at least one doctor, a GP is allocated by the FPC. However this allocation is for only two weeks, and the health visitors are concerned about the quality of treatment where the doctor has been assigned a patient.

One GP felt that she and two other GP practices in the area saw a disproportionate number of homeless, not necessarily because they were particularly close to the hotel but because they were more sympathetic to the homeless. She explained, "The GP down the road just will not see homeless families at all — he likes private practice too much. You see the problem is that homeless families have a lot of kids and are just generally not acceptable. You do not want people like that in your surgery, as you have wealthy patients with mink coats."

In Manchester health visitors also felt that homeless families had difficulty gaining access to GPs near the hotels. One health visitor explained: "One woman came to see me and said that a local GP will not let her go on his list. I phoned up the GP and asked if I could go on his list — as though I was an ordinary local resident. He said I could. So I asked why he had not accepted the homeless family. Then he agreed to take them on."

While the two GPs who were approached for this study in Manchester denied that they discriminated against the homeless, this was difficult to establish because they both said that they did not have time to discuss the matter. However midwives in Manchester did perceive a problem. In South Manchester one hospital has responded by allowing pregnant women to book into the antenatal clinic even if they have no letter from a GP, which is usually required.

In Manchester a specialist in community medicine (housing) has been appointed by the city council. Recognising that there may be a problem with access to GPs, he has asked the homeless families' health visitors to provide information on families who find it difficult to register. He then contacts the relevant Family Practitioner Committee and asks for a GP to be assigned. As he points out, this is not a "definitive solution", because "it denies families choice of GPs; the process is stigmatising; is unlikely to foster good doctor-patient relationships; and it is very labour-intensive."

So far, just over ten patients have been assigned — a possible indication that access to GPs is not such a problem in Manchester. Before patients are assigned, however, they may already have been refused by several GPs.

Despite the impression given by health visitors in Southend, the doctor interviewed there did not feel that GPs were reluctant to see homeless families. He suggested that at the moment "our lists are full. But if we were accepting patients we should accept the homeless as much as anyone else. There can be no reason, and it would be wrong to discriminate between different people because of the life they are leading. We are not here to be moral judges."

As shown in Chapter 4 in relation to services for pregnant women, people are at an even greater disadvantage when their first language is not English. The Bangladeshi women in the survey seemed to have particular problems finding a local doctor because they had been placed in a hotel far away from their own community and could not find a Bengali-speaking doctor near the hotel. This applies to many of the families in Bayswater, London, placed there by Tower Hamlets Council, and to families in Hounslow, West London.

People who move frequently are also at a disadvantage because it takes on average six weeks for medical records to be transferred from one GP to another: therefore homeless families may often seek treatment from a doctor who does not yet hold their records.

The Health Visitors Association and the British Medical Association are now working together to improve health care for families in hotels. They are jointly producing a leaflet for primary health care professionals including GP's suggesting practical ways in which the services could be made more available and more useful to hotel residents.

Organising GP services

The health services in Finsbury Park, London, have made a special effort to meet the needs of families in hotels. They have designated one GP "with special interest in homelessness". She explained that "the Community Health Council produced critical reports of the health centre — on the building, reception and the services that should be provided. They, for example, made us realise that we needed a full-time Bangladeshi health worker."

The CHC also put pressure on the FPC. With the help of an enlightened administrator, the FPC was able to encourage all the local GPs to take on homeless families and agree to register homeless patients permanently from day one. The GP with special interest in the homeless felt this had worked well. "Homeless families are seen by all the GPs in this clinic, together with a local partnership and two single-handed GPs. In this area, unlike Bayswater, you would have difficulty finding a homeless family who is not signed on with a GP."

The largest homeless hotel in the country is in Hounslow, where a GP has held a surgery for the last three years. Initially he registers all the families as temporary patients. In a year he sees about

600 homeless people as temporary patients and a further 300 who are registered permanently. The number of homeless families in the hotel has grown from 60 people to over 750 in just three years. To meet their health needs, the GP holds two surgeries a week in the hotel, an antenatal clinic every fortnight and a vaccination clinic every month.

Because of the large number of families living there, a health visitor is based permanently at the hotel. There is also a multi-disciplinary professionals' group that includes the GP, midwives, health visitors, environmental health officers and local headmistresses. The GP finds this group very useful and recommends it for other areas with a concentration of hotel homeless. His main source of frustration is that he "can't get them out of the hotels. I can't solve their housing problems. I can write letters if they have severe medical problems, but I can only shift them up a point or two on the waiting list. I don't even have the time to counsel them".

Problems with primary health care: health visitors and midwives

Health visitors and midwives are frequently the first, and sometimes the only, representatives of statutory or advisory bodies to contact homeless families in bed and breakfast hotels and are in a unique position to detail the effects of hotel life on health.

Caseloads

The rise in homelessness in London, Southend and Manchester means that many of the health visitors interviewed for this survey work exclusively with homeless families in hotels.

In Bayswater, three health visitors visit nearly 430 families, two of whom work exclusively with those in hotels; Finsbury Park has two homeless health visitors whose caseload never drops below 300 families; Manchester has two specialist health visitors with a combined caseload of 250 families; and in Southend two health visitors see nearly 250 homeless — a third of their total caseload. All the health visitors suggested that these very large numbers make it impossible to provide a comprehensive service.

In Manchester, the specialist health visitors can cope only with the families who have been placed in hotels by the council — other hotel families who have not been accepted as homeless or declared intentionally homeless are not visited. One of the specialist health visitors explained: "We would need one health visitor per 50 families if we were to find and visit families we are not seeing at the moment."

In Bayswater, the two specialist health visitor posts were created by moving existing health visitors, not by creating additional posts. Not surprisingly, a local paediatrician has received complaints from local mothers that they are now getting an inadequate service. There is also an argument that hotel homeless families require extra resources because of their particular needs. Black people are over-represented amongst the hotel homeless, but health authorities do not appear to recognise the double disadvantage faced by ethnic minorities. Bayswater has a Sylheti interpreter for four sessions a week, but the health visitor feels that more resources are needed if there is to be a proper health programme for Bangladeshi families. The local paediatrician often resorts to communicating with mothers through their husbands, which she feels puts both the mothers and her at a disadvantage, and means that a second-rate service is provided.

Caseloads were also an issue amongst the midwives in Bayswater. One midwife started working in 1972 when there were virtually no homeless families in the area. Now she has a very heavy caseload, visiting an average of 15 to 17 homeless families per day.

A health visitor in Bloomsbury summarised the feelings of many of the health workers: "As a health visitor my priority might be to focus on issues such as safety, an adequate diet, or the stimulation of the child, but to the parent the health visitor is seen as someone who may have an influence in the housing department or the DHSS. When, in the majority of cases, it is explained that there is little you can actually do, your credibility is lost, and anything else you can offer, such as clinic facilities, information on access to health care, or advice on child care issues is a poor second best for the client. It's easy to see why they quickly lose interest. One constantly feels the need to apologise to people for the things you are unable to do."

Lack of information

In Southend and London families are often placed in hotels that are outside the area of the housing authority that has accepted them as homeless. Very often health visitors do not know of a family's arrival in a hotel unless they come across them while on their rounds.

In Southend health visitors see families from Basildon, Castlepoint and Rochford as well as Southend. Neither Southend Council nor other placing councils contact the health visitors to tell them when they are placing families in hotels — despite representations from the health visitors.

For over five years there has been an Association of London Authorities (ALA) and London Boroughs Association (LBA) code of practice on the use of hotels.[1] Although it includes procedures for notification between homeless persons units and health workers in receiving boroughs, health visitors in Bayswater and Finsbury Park found that the system did not work.

In Bayswater, health visitors initially contacted homeless persons units in each placing borough. This was abandoned as numbers increased. Only two placing boroughs now provide any information to the health visitors and that often two or three months after the family has moved in. "By that time," a health visitor explained, "we have invariably already found the family by trawling the hotels."

Bayswater is in Westminster, and the health visitors do get weekly lists from the borough when placing their own families. However the information supplied includes everyone placed in hotels by the council, with no indication of their ages to guide the health visitors towards families with children.

Besides visiting each individual hotel to find new families, health visitors discover a small percentage through contacts with other workers. Some families are referred by hospitals because there is a new baby or they have had an illness, and sometimes a social worker or health visitor from another borough may contact the health visitors because they are worried about a family. However relatively few contacts are made this way.

Finsbury Park has the second largest concentration of families in hotels in London. One borough, Islington, does provide regular information on new families placed in the hotels including dates of birth, information on where the family has come from, and if the woman is pregnant. But other boroughs provide none. Like their colleagues in Bayswater, health visitors in Finsbury Park have to rely on time-consuming door-knocking to find new families.

It is a matter of great concern that all the health visitors interviewed were worried that they could not cope with the homeless families they already had contact with. Referral procedures need to be improved and more information supplied between boroughs. However if this were to happen without additional resources, then health visitors' ability to provide an adequate service to the homeless would be even further diminished.

Local initiatives to improve health care

In order to improve access to health care several initiatives have been tried by health authorities. A Steering Group for homeless families has been set up in Manchester with representation from the city council, the health authorities and interested non-statutory agencies. The Steering Group is looking at, among other things, ways of improving access to GPs for hotel homeless families. The Group is also looking further ahead and considering alternative forms of temporary accommodation for homeless families.

In Finsbury Park, a "health mobile" for homeless families operates every Monday and a playgroup is being established in the neighbouring church hall. The mobile van aims to offer some health provision for homeless people who are not attending the local clinic and is staffed by a Bangladeshi health worker, two health visitors and a GP. It has its limitations due to the lack of space, but a senior registrar at the local department of community medicine feels that it has been a success. It gives homeless people easy access to health care services and they are more likely to keep follow-up appointments at the clinic. The child health clinic that was held in the mobile has now been moved into the health centre.

"Since starting the mobile we have immunised over three hundred children — and that's three hundred more than would have been immunised if the mobile was not available."

In Bayswater, the idea of a health mobile was rejected, as it was felt that it would mean that homeless families would be provided with health care in the same cramped conditions that they were forced to live in. Instead, health visitors wanted to develop the homeless families' playgroup into a multi-disciplinary centre where proper health care would be provided with child care, welfare benefit and housing advice, and social work support. Some housing and welfare advice sessions are already being run at the playgroup. In addition a multi-disciplinary group has been established to provide for the health care of the homeless. However there has been no increase in the number of health visitors and the specialist visitors can only undertake priority visits — to new births and disabled children. Everyone else has to go to the increasingly overcrowded clinic. As one health visitor pointed out: "It has taken us three years to establish this team — now it's too little, too late."

The health workers have mixed feelings about the provision of specialist health workers. Whilst it provides health visitors who are sympathetic to the needs of the homeless it is an extremely stressful job and providing separate specialist services may marginalise these families.

These contradictions are well illustrated by events in Bloomsbury. In Bloomsbury it was hoped to develop a team of health workers for homeless families. In the event, only two additional specialist health visitors was appointed, and one of them stayed in the post for only three months. The other health visitor carried on working by herself for a further five months until she resigned. She felt that neither the present system nor specialist health visitors were the correct response to hotel homelessness. Rather, in the short term, responsibility for homeless families should be shared among all health visitors becaue of the stress the work involves. This could be effective only if additional resources and clerical support were provided.

Health centres for the single homeless have been established in several cities and the experiences there indicate some of the issues that may arise if specialist provision is considered for homeless families. Recent articles and reports have pointed to some of the problems associated with such centres — even though they may provide a sympathetic service to the homeless.[2]

Specialist centres can make local GPs feel that they are absolved from responsibility for the homeless. In Manchester, one of the GPs was critical of the appointment of a salaried GP to provide health care specifically for single homeless people: "The introduction of the salaried GP actually removed some of the single homeless from general health care, because they were previously registered with GPs. After the system was introduced, some GPs may have assumed that the homeless were no longer their problem." The reported reluctance of some GPs to see homeless people needs to be tackled directly.

Experience from single homeless projects indicates that specialist facilities rarely provide a 24-hour, seven-day service and they could never cover the needs of the homeless throughout the country. Also, most centres can only obtain funding if the homeless are treated as temporary or emergency patients — making full case records unavailable.

By channelling all the homeless to one source of general medical care, specialist centres are effectively denying the right of patients to choose their GP. If relationships between patient and specialist practitioner break down, it is the patient who is left stranded.

In their report on specialist health provision for the single homeless, the Health Sub-Group of the Joint Working Party on Single Homelessness in London (SHIL) made various recommendations to improve primary health care for single homeless people that are also of direct relevance to homeless families.[3] One key recommendation is the introduction of salaried general practitioners for *everyone* in inner cities. This would inhibit the abuse of the current capitation method of payment, and recognise the liaison work that inner city GPs should be involved in if they are to service the community effectively.

SHIL also suggests that in order to integrate the homeless within primary health care services, health development workers should be employed by district health authorities, and health liaison workers by family practitioners committees, and also workers should be appointed to research and monitor the co-ordination of health care issues. Although such appointments clearly have resource implications, they would allow primary health care provision to be more effective and more efficiently targeted.

If there is still a desire to create specialist facilities for homeless families, the environmental health visitor in Bloomsbury has a warning. "By providing special services and facilities for the homeless," she says, "we are tacitly condoning a system that accepts and allows people to become homeless, and will continue to do so as long as buffers are provided which take the edge off the situation."

REFERENCES

1 "Joint London Boroughs Code of Practice: The use of hotel/hostel accommodation for the placement of homeless people: Code of Guidance", London Boroughs Association/Association of London Authorities. 1986.
2 "Primary Health Care for Single Homeless People in London: a strategic approach", Report of the Health Sub-Group of the Joint Working Party on Single Homelessness in London. January 1987.
   Jonathan Stearn, "No home, no health care", *Roof* Magazine, May/June 1987.
3 Health Sub-Group of the Joint Working Party on Single Homelessness in London. *op. cit.*

Young mother with recently born infant.
Bed and Breakfast hotel. Finsbury Park, London. October, 1987.

CHAPTER 8

Environmental health action on hotel standards

Introduction and summary

THERE IS a range of powers and duties available to local authorities to enforce better standards in Houses in Multiple Occupation (HMOs) which includes hotels used by homeless people. The main powers and duties are:

♦ to require additional amenities and facilities (such as WCs and bathrooms);

♦ to fix a limit on the number of people living in the building, to prevent overcrowding (a "direction order");

♦ to require the provision of adequate means of escape in case of fire or closing part of the building;

♦ to require the landlord to comply with a code of management (a "management order"). In

extreme cases the local authority can take over the management of the building (a "control order"), backed up by a "compulsory purchase order";
- ♦ to require HMOs to register;
- ♦ to provide special grants for improvements and repairs;
- ♦ to enforce health and safety standards for people working on the premises.

For this study environmental health officers (EHOs) in all three study areas (including two London boroughs) were interviewed about their policies and practices in relation to standards in hotels for the homeless. In most cases the officers felt frustrated by the scale of the problem and their lack of adequate resources and powers. However one council, Camden, did seem to be more successful in using its powers. The Institute of Environmental Health Officers has suggested that there are three main reasons for the failure to enforce standards: the lack of local authority resources; the complexity of the legislation; and the lack of will to tackle the problem.

This study supports the view that current resources are inadequate to tackle the enormous problems in hotels. In terms of the law, a number of attempts have been made to introduce new legislation to improve standards in HMOs including hotels; however all have failed through lack of government support. It seems that the will to improve standards in what must be amongst the very worst type of housing in this country is lacking at both central and local government level.

Environmental health practices in the study areas

Westminster

WESTMINSTER COUNCIL serves notices for overcrowding and management at the rate of 50-60 per year on Houses in Multiple Occupation, approximately a quarter of which are on bed and breakfast hotels. With the exception of cooking facilities, Westminster's standards are based on the London Boroughs Association/Association of London Authorities Code of Practice on the use of hotels.[1] The Council seems to be reasonably happy with the action they are taking and their powers of enforcement. Their main complaint is that court procedures take too long and fines on hoteliers are insufficient.

However, the Council's policy on HMOs has not been without its critics. On the 20th November 1984, a homeless mother and her two small children died in a fire in a hotel in Gloucester Place, Westminster, where the family had been placed by Camden Council. At the inquest, the jury recorded an open verdict, but took the unusual step of commenting that "we feel inadequate fire precautions and means of escape greatly contributed to the deaths". It was admitted that there had been a breakdown in communications within various departments in Westminster and between Westminster Council and the then fire authority — the Greater London Council.

Following the inquest several internal changes were made, and the Environmental Health Department is now responsible for means of escape in case of fire. It is the Environmental Health Department which now liaises with the London Fire and Civil Defence Authority.

There were two more fire deaths in an HMO in Westminster in 1986, and independent environmental health officers again criticised the fire standards enforced by Westminster Council. Although the Council did not accept the report's findings, they nevertheless decided to employ four more environmental health officers to reduce the period between inspections on HMOs from four years to two years; however these inspections are for means of escape only. The Council now aims to carry out full inspection of hotels for the homeless at least four times a year.

Camden

The fire in Westminster in 1984 also encouraged Camden Council to employ more EHOs, and to change the responsibilities of council departments. Prior to the fire, three EHOs inspected hotels within the borough and another inspected hotels used by Camden outside the borough. Following the fire two additional EHOs were appointed to make a total complement of six environmental health officers, one technical officer and one administrative officer inspecting hotels inside and outside the borough. But according to the officers, even this level of staffing is inadequate.

The environmental health officers started by inspecting the 73 hotels used to accommodate homeless people accepted by the Council. They found that none was suitable for use by families or single people — over 20 were totally "unsuitable and not capable of improvement to any standard." By the middle of 1986 the Council had stopped using all the hotels that they considered to be a health risk.

A full range of Housing Act notices were served on 50 of the remaining hotels. However these were not thoroughly followed up because the officers had to turn their attention to a large number of additional hotels which the Council wanted to use to meet the rapidly rising numbers of homeless families. (Hotels have to be passed by the EHOs before they can be used for Camden's homeless families.) The Environmental Health Department is also having to deal with other boroughs choosing to use hotels that have been approved by Camden.

Camden's experience is that the threat of withdrawal of trade has encouraged all the hotels who have been served notices to carry out the works required before court proceedings are instigated. Camden, unlike Westminster, also accepts the cooking standards in the LBA/ALA Code[2]. According to the Camden EHOs, "It is no big deal getting them to put catering facilities in, if you can convince the hotelier that the trade is there. A problem only tends to arise if the hotelier has hotels in other boroughs and argues that those councils are not forcing these improvements on them."

Camden also seems more determined than some councils to push hard for improvements in the face of opposition. One large hotel that had been subject to notices proved particularly reluctant to comply with the Council's demands. "They put up a concerted case, involving solicitors and a barrister. They appealed against our notices. But we held firm all the time and made it clear that we were 100 per cent confident of our action and we were going to follow it through, come what may. They were looking at delaying for at least eighteen months before we came to court. So we sent in food inspectors and health and safety specialists and served Public Health and Building Act Notices. Eventually they complied because they could not handle it any more." Another key reason for their success in this case was liaison with the other boroughs who were using the hotel. That took considerable time and effort and could not be repeated on every case without increased staff resources.

Manchester

Shortage of environmental health officers is also an issue in Manchester. The Council recently introduced new standards for the two and a half thousand HMOs in the city, yet the EHOs feel there are not enough of them to enforce the standards. "Our problem has always been staffing levels," said one environmental health officer. "We have not been able to work any rolling programme. We have only been able to respond to complaints when they arise. That is obviously not satisfactory, but it's all we have been able to do."

When Manchester introduced the new standards, landlords were asked to comply voluntarily within two years. Although at the time of the interviews for this study the period was nearly up, the environmental health officers reported that very few landlords had come forward.

A steering group of health visitors, social workers and environmental health officers has been established to try to monitor new hotels. If the property is not self-contained flats, the environmental health officer does not give approval for use. "I am not saying that always works," said the EHO. "The housing department has still gone into hotels where I have said 'no' — even though they have made various undertakings that they would reduce the level of use of bed and breakfast."

There is a growing realisation that as the numbers of homeless in bed and breakfast hotels increases, more effective measures will have to be taken to enforce the new standards for cooking facilities and other amenities in the hotels. If necessary powers to reduce overcrowding will be used to create the space for the extra facilities. "We are reluctant to serve section 352 notices on hotels (requiring additional amenities and facilities) because they are entitled to a special grant. This council is not keen to pay a special grant to a hotel owner who is already being paid what we consider to be exorbitant rates for housing homeless families."

Southend

Tower Hamlets Council's decision to place homeless Bangladeshi families in hotels in Southend in 1985 led to the establishment of an HMO working party in Southend which published a report in February 1986.[3] This recommended the appointment of one additional environmental health officer and a technical assistant, and proposed that the areas with the highest concentration of HMOs should be the main focus for action on standards and conditions.

Six were designated, and work of inspecting every house used for homeless people in each area started in October 1986. This was a change from the previous policy of inspecting HMOs only when complaints were received. However, with existing staffing levels and an improved code of standards for HMOs, environmental health officers estimate that it will take some six to eight years to inspect and take action on the six areas so far designated — let alone to start inspecting four other areas with a lower concentration of HMOs.

To contain the proliferation of HMOs, the working party also suggested changes in planning policy. It was decided to give "favourable consideration" to planning applications for HMOs which would provide self-contained accommodation with a "demonstrable degree of management and supervision".[4] The Council also decided to insist on one parking space per bedroom and, where appropriate, to require the "provision for managers' accommodation and cooking, dining room and communal lounge facilities within the premises".[5] In this way it was hoped to control the spread of bed and breakfast establishments.

Southend Environmental Health Department has never used control orders to take over the day-to-day management of HMOs. The department believes that the legislation is too cumbersome, it takes too much staff time, and objects to the possibility of paying landlords for loss of income. This contrasts with Camden officers who believe that the use of control orders against one landlord encourages others to improve standards of management and conditions.

Some 200 HMOs in Southend were informally encouraged to improve conditions in 1986/87, yet only 11 notices were served to enforce proper means of escape from fire, with only five notices for improved amenities.

Although the chief environmental health officer in Southend was reluctant to say how many extra staff were needed, it is clear that the existing officers face an uphill task. At the time of the interviews there were still over 160 known unauthorised HMOs to visit. As the 1981 census identified 2,068 shared households in Southend there must be a considerable number of HMOs yet to be discovered.

Limitations on local authority action

The evidence of local authority environmental health action in the study areas suggests that councils are not adequately coping with the problems of hotel standards. The Institution of Environmental Health Officers (IEHO) has suggested that the low level of activity on HMOs might be explained by the complexity of the legislation, lack of resources within local authorities, and the lack of concern for conditions within what is usually the worst part of the private rented sector.[6]

One independent environmental health officer interviewed for this study felt that his fellow professionals were reluctant to enforce standards. "Fire is the most pressing issue that environmental health officers have to consider — it is the major attack on health you can have in a hotel. Yet because of the ambiguity between the environmental health department and the fire authority, environmental health officers are frequently lax when using their powers to enforce protective staircases, emergency lighting, alarms, secondary means of escape and the like. There is a major gulf between what is asked for and what really should be demanded if environmental health officers had the safety of residents as their primary concern."

The same environmental health officer felt that his colleagues did not appreciate and properly evaluate the special problems faced by people living in one room. "They should realise that a broken window or damp in the only room you have to live in is very different from the same fault in a room when a family has a whole house to live in." This EHO felt that environmental health officers are too influenced by council pressures to approve the use of unsatisfactory accommodation because of the housing shortage and do not enforce the standards they should. In his view they should be complaining to the IEHO that they are being prevented from conducting their work according to the Code of Professional Practice.

That local authorities lack resources to implement standards properly was highlighted as a major problem by nearly all the environmental health officers interviewed for this study. It is felt that additional enforcement officers are needed. However the interviews suggest that, given government restrictions on council spending, councils will only commit extra resources if legislation is introduced to make the enforcement of minimum standards and conditions mandatory.

To help ease the situation the IEHO has suggested that, in some cases, councils could obtain funding under Section 11 of the Local Government Act 1966 to employ staff specifically to meet the needs of black and ethnic minorities who are over-represented amongst the hotel homeless.[7] Up to 75 per cent of the salaries for such staff can be paid by the Home Office. Although some authorities have used Section 11 funding to employ extra staff, community groups have sometimes criticised this because it should not be seen as a marginal part of local authority provision.

The need for government action

The IEHO feels that the legislation surrounding the enforcement of standards in HMOs (including hotels) is too complex.

An example of this is the law on fire safety as it affects hotels in London. Hotels and boarding houses need a fire certificate enforced by the fire authority under the Fire Precautions Act 1971. It is mandatory for means of escape in hotels in outer London to be enforced by the local authority under Section 72, Building Act 1984. In inner London, hotels built since 1940 should have means of escape as a mandatory enforced duty by the fire authority under the London Building Act 1939, Section 34. Conversely, for hotels in inner London built before 1940 the enforcement of means of escape from fire is at the discretion of the authority. A draft national standard for fire protection was only recently been produced by the Home Office in late 1987.[8]

Since 1979, several bills to control standards in HMOs have been introduced in both houses of Parliament but the Government has failed to support any of these initiatives. The most recent was introduced by Brian Wilson in February 1988. This was almost identical to the bill introduced by Donald Anderson in 1987.

These bills aimed to:

♦ place a duty on councils to locate and regularly inspect all HMOs in their area;
♦ place a duty on councils to ensure that all HMOs have adequate means of escape from fire;
♦ establish national minimum standards for HMOs and place a duty on authorities to enforce them;
♦ streamline the procedures by which councils can take over the worst HMOs (by using control orders). Harassment would be included as grounds for taking control of an HMO;
♦ enable tenants to initiate action to improve conditions in their home;
♦ give HMO residents the right to rehousing if they are made homeless as a result of local authority action to improve conditions.

Without a strong government commitment to improve standards in HMOs, hotel residents are dependent on environmental health officers using their existing powers to safeguard the health of residents. The IEHO has recently started producing a regular newsheet on HMOs which may increase knowledge of successful practices. This study suggests that imagination and a determination to take action *can* improve conditions in hotels — despite the lack of resources and complexity of the legislation. Many councils do not show the will to achieve this.

The IEHO has commented: "Whilst the powers to deal with the problems are, in the main, available now, the legislation needs considerable rationalisation, and recalcitrant local authorities have to be pushed into facing up to the need for action."[9]

REFERENCES

1. "Joint London Boroughs Code of Practice: The use of hotel/hostel accommodation for the placement of homeless people: Code of guidance", London Boroughs Association/Association of London Authorities. 1986.
2. *Ibid.*
3. "Houses in Multiple occupation". A report of a working party established by Southend District Council, February 1986.
4. *Op. cit*
5. *Op. cit*
   "Houses in Multiple Occupation". A report of a working party established by the Institution of Environmental Health Officers. May 1985.
7. "Race and Environmental health". A joint report produced by the Institution of Environmental Health Officers and the Commission for Racial Equality. October 1984.
8. "Draft guide to means of escape and related fire safety measures in certain HMOs". Home Office. 1987.
9. "Houses in multiple occupation", The report of a working party established by the Institution of Environmental Health Officers. 1985.

Credit: The Morning Star

B & B families lobby the DoE. July 1987. London.

Summary

Introduction

WHAT HOMELESS families need most is suitable permanent housing at a price they can afford. Few people live in temporary accommodation through choice, and bed and breakfast hotels could never be seen as adequate housing. They are totally unsuitable as homes for families with young children and are an extremely expensive form of housing. This study set out to discover whether conditions in bed and breakfast hotels are unhealthy, whether the health of mothers and children suffers and whether their access to health services is affected by their living in a hotel.

A common concern with the effects of bed and breakfast living on the increasing numbers of homeless pregnant women, mothers and their young children living in hotels has brought together the four organisations involved in this report. Combining expertise in housing, health and diet, the study was carried out in four parts:

♦ interviews with 57 women living in bed and breakfast hotels about their own and their children's health;

♦ a detailed analysis of the diets of 48 of these women and an investigation of the children's diets;

♦ interviews with GPs, health visitors, midwives and environmental health officers;

♦ an analysis of the health records for women and children living in hotels compared with similar people not living in hotels.

The bed and breakfast crisis

The amount of new housing to rent being built by local authorities and housing associations has dropped by over 80 per cent in the last ten years, and it has therefore become more and more difficult for many people to find a permanent home. Increasing numbers of pregnant women and families with children find that the only home available to them for months and sometimes years is a hotel room. Well over 11,000 households are now living in hotels, including a high proportion of families with children.

Conditions in the 38 hotels covered by this survey can only be described as appalling. Nearly half the households were estimated as being overcrowded in terms of the law. Many of the children had to share their beds with an adult, and the bedrooms often had no space for a table or chairs. Most families had to share the WC and bathroom, sometimes with a large number of other people. Hotels were often dirty and conditions unhygienic. The mothers were particularly worried about the lack of safety in hotels, including both physical dangers and the lack of privacy and of control over halls and stairways. This sense of insecurity exacerbates the stress of living in a hotel.

Although the women in the survey had already been living in hotels for some time, with a third having been there for over a year, most did not know how much longer they would be living in a hotel, or expected to be there at least another year.

While ultimately homelessness can only be tackled by providing more homes, the 11,000 or more households now living in hotels may have to wait a long time before getting a permanent home. This report focuses on their needs, and the needs of those who will be living in hotels in the future.

Women's health

Interviews carried out with 57 women in a range of hotels in London, Manchester and Southend revealed a high level of stress and illness amongst the women and their children. Tension and depression were common, and many women felt very isolated, often spending long periods of time each day in cramped bedrooms. Family relationships often became strained. Both the women and their children seemed to become ill frequently, particularly with severe headaches, chest infections, diarrhoea and sickness. The families in this study had very little money to spend: most were unemployed and those in work were earning very low wages. Yet hotel life is itself expensive and many were having to go without basic necessities, including food. This is likely to have a bad effect on health — both by increasing their worries and restricting their diet.

Twenty-seven of the women interviewed had been pregnant while living in an hotel, or were pregnant at the time of the interview. The stresses of hotel life and the difficulties of getting proper meals particularly affect pregnant women. Over half mentioned problems during their pregnancy such as high blood pressure. Many were aware of the detrimental effect of their inadequate diet. The midwives and health visitors interviewed shared these concerns and the analysis of women's health records in Manchester showed that women who were homeless during their pregnancy were more likely to have had problems and to have been admitted to hospital during the pregnancy. Babies born to mothers in homeless hotels were more likely to have been born prematurely or with a low birthweight.

The women's food and diets

In general, the quality of the diets of the women in the survey was poor, and seemed, where comparisons were possible, to compare unfavourably with that of other people with low incomes in the general population.

Breakfast was often not provided and if it was, was frequently at an inconvenient time, or was inedible. Over one third of the women hardly ever prepared a meal for their families, and a quarter ate take-away foods more than four times a week. They tended to eat fewer vegetables than people with poor incomes generally — and this is already considerably lower than the amount eaten by those with higher incomes. Those women who had to cut back on food or sometimes go without for financial reasons tended also to have the poorest diets.

The lack of adequate kitchen and food storage facilities were found to be important influences on the quality of the women's diets. In many cases there was nowhere suitable to store food, and fresh food had to be bought daily. Where kitchens did exist, they were often two or more floors away from the bedroom, overcrowded, dirty, and considered by the women to be dangerous. Only four of the 57 women had access to kitchens which met the standards for bed and breakfast accommodation laid down by the Association of London Authorities.

Some women had kettles and kitchen equipment in the bedrooms, but were concerned about the safety of their children — burns were not uncommon. Six of the women had no means at all of preparing any hot food or drinks. Because of the lack of kitchen facilities, many of them were reliant on take-away and cafe food. This tends to be more expensive than home-cooked food.

The women were, on the whole, fairly unhappy about their diets and the way in which they felt forced to feed their children. The vast majority felt that they had eaten better before they moved into hotels. The inability to provide adequate food for themselves and their families was a source of stress for the women.

The health of the children

A high incidence of illness was reported among the 71 pre-school children in the survey. Mothers also highlighted the behavioural problems their children had developed since moving to a hotel — such as sleeping and eating badly, being unusually aggressive or wild, or bed-wetting.

The health professionals interviewed voiced similar anxieties about epidemics of infectious illnesses, about delays in the children's development and about the generally poor health of homeless women and children.

These findings are underlined by the evidence from the analysis of infant health records. This clearly shows some of the ways in which the health of homeless mothers and babies is at risk, even in areas where local health authorities are making strenuous efforts to provide for their particular needs. The high incidence of low birthweight among homeless babies is one of the most striking findings in this report. It is not argued here that bed and breakfast living *causes* low birthweight; there is, however, ample evidence in this report to suggest that it may contribute to it.

Infant health records detail immunisations and vaccinations given, and the gaps in the records of homeless infants were substantial. As many as half the Manchester children had missed out on at least one immunisation, and access to these preventive health measures was far less common amongst homeless infants in London than amongst those who were not homeless. A similar picture emerged from the analysis of developmental assessment records. In Manchester a third of the children had missed the assessment due at one year, as had three-quarters of the homeless children in London.

On the evidence of this report, homeless children living in bed and breakfast hotels are at a disadvantage in terms of health. They are less likely to grow and develop skills as quickly as other children and are more susceptible to illnesses.

Health and environmental health services

In spite of the evidence of stress and illness among hotel families, they seem to have poor access to health services. Many had found it difficult to register with a local doctor and some doctors seem reluctant to take on hotel residents. A significant proportion of the children were not even getting regular visits from the health visitor.

Health professionals were often well aware of the inadequate service they were able to offer homeless families and some attempts are being made to improve the services. However all health services were under-resourced to cope with the special needs of the homeless. Health visitors sometimes had intolerable caseloads, and many staff felt isolated and ill-informed. Their frustration was increased by knowing that they had no power to provide the one thing families wanted and needed — a permanent home.

Environmental health action by local authorities to improve standards in hotels was found by this study to be extremely limited. This may be partly due to the lack of local authority resources, especially staff, and the complexity and limitations of the legislation. However this study also suggests it may reflect a lack of will by both central and local government to tackle seriously some of the worst housing problems in this country.

What this report shows

This survey is an indictment of hotel life. It shows that pregnant women, mothers and young children are living in totally unfit housing, often with little support from housing or health services and with no idea of when they will be rehoused.

It shows, too, that women's and children's health is badly affected by the conditions and stresses of having to live for long periods of time in totally unsuitable circumstances. The lack of decent kitchen facilities means that most women cannot provide their families with the basic necessities of life, such as a healthy meal. The response of Central Government, local councils and health services seems to be grossly inadequate to meet their needs.

Among the homeless children whose health records were studied, one in five of those in London and one in seven of those in Manchester was less than six months old. Many had spent all of their short lives in bed and breakfast hotels. In London, some children had lived in bed and breakfast until they were two years old, without ever knowing a real home. These are some of the most vulnerable children born in this country and their good health is seriously at risk.

Appendix 1
Questionnaire for women in bed and breakfast

QUESTIONNAIRE FOR WOMEN IN BED AND BREAKFAST

SECTION 1 - CONTACT SHEET

1. Name ....   Case no: [ ]
2. Address ....   Area Code: [ ]
   ....
   ....

   Interviewer's Name ....
   Referred by ....

Contacts:	1st	2nd	3rd
date			
time of day			
no reply			
refusal			
appointment made			
need interpreter			
other problems			
partial interview			
full interview			

   Sections completed: 3 and 4 [ ]   tick
   6 [ ]   as
   7 [ ]   appropriate
   8 [ ]

   Interviewer's general impressions (space/furniture/hazards/approach to room etc).

   - 1 -

SECTION 2. HOUSEHOLD DETAILS

Office Code

3. Firstly of all, can you tell me who lives here with you? [Include all who live here only.]

Relationship	Sex	Age
Women	F	

   Household type [ ]

   No. of people [ ]

4. How old are you/are they? (complete above)

SECTION 3. CHILDRENS' HEALTH

IF NO CHILD, GO TO SECTION 5

   Child aged:
   1) 1-2 2-3 3-4 4-5

Now I want to ask about your childrens' health.

5. Does ... [NAME] have any long-term health problem? (e.g. asthma, eczema) [write who and what]

6. Has s/he had any of the following illnesses since living in a hotel?
   - chest infections?   1 1 1 1 1   ring
   - diarrhoea?   2 2 2 2 2   mo(re)
   - sickness/vomiting?   3 3 3 3 3   tha(n)
   - bladder/kidney infections? 4 4 4 4 4 one
   - burns or scalds?   5 5 5 5 5
   - accidents (bad falls or cuts)? 6 6 6 6 6
   - any other illnesses? [write in] 7 7 7 7 7

   - 2 -

---

7. Would you say s/he often has any of the following problems:

   Child aged:
   1) 1-2 2-3 3-4 4-5

   - very bad at sleeping?   1 1 1 1 1   ring
   - persistent bedwetting?   2 2 2 2 2   more
   - major eating problems?   3 3 3 3 3   than
   - unusually quiet/passive/listless? 4 4 4 4 4 one
   - unusually aggressive/active?   5 5 5 5 5
   - any other problems? [write]   6 6 6 6 6

8. Would you say her/his health is generally better, worse or about the same since moving into a hotel?
   - better   1 1 1 1 1
   - worse   2 2 2 2 2
   - the same   3 3 3 3 3
   - NA if born in hotel   4 4 4 4 4

   IF BETTER OR WORSE: In what way? [write]

9. If s/he is ill enough to need help, where would you usually go?
   - GP   1 1 1 1 1   ring
   - health visitor   2 2 2 2 2   more
   - clinic/health centre   3 3 3 3 3   than
   - hospital   4 4 4 4 4   one
   - other [write]   5 5 5 5 5
   - DK   6 6 6 6 6

   IF CLINIC/HEALTH CENTRE: Who do you see there? [If GP or health visitor, Code 1 or 2]

   - 3 -

---

10. Are you happy with this or not?

    Child aged:
    1) 1-2 2-3 3-4 4-5

    - yes   1 1 1 1 1
    - no   2 2 2 2 2
    - DK   3 3 3 3 3

    IF NO: What are the problems? [write]

11. Is s/he registered with a GP?
    - no   1 1 1 1 1   ring
    - yes - in this area, temporarily   2 2 2 2 2   more
    - yes - in this area, permanently   3 3 3 3 3   than
    - yes - in previous area   4 4 4 4 4   one
    - other [write]   5 5 5 5 5
    - DK   6 6 6 6 6

    PROBE: TEMPORARILY OR PERMANENTLY THIS AND PREVIOUS AREA

12. Have you had any difficulties getting him/her registered with a GP in this area?
    - no   1 1 1 1 1
    - yes   2 2 2 2 2
    - not tried 3 3 3 3 3
    - DK   4 4 4 4 4
    [write]

13. Have you had to take her/him to a hospital since living in a hotel?
    - no   1 1 1 1 1
    - yes - inpatient   2 2 2 2 2   more
    - yes - outpatient 3 3 3 3 3   than
    - yes - casualty   4 4 4 4 4   one
    - DK

    IF YES: How many times?
    What was this for?
    [write]

    IF CASUALTY: What time of day was this?

    - 4 -

Questionnaire for women in bed and breakfast

```
                                    Child aged:
                                    1) 1-2  2-3  3-4  4-5
```

Do you have a health visitor?
- yes   Y Y Y Y Y
- no   1 1 1 1 1
- DK   7 7 7 7 7

IF YES: Does the health visitor ever come to visit you?
- no, never   2 2 2 2 2
- yes, rarely/once only   3 3 3 3 3
- yes, sometimes   4 4 4 4 4
- yes, regularly   5 5 5 5 5
- DK   6 6 6 6 6

IF YES: Where do you see her?
[write]

How long after you moved into a hotel, or after the baby was born, did she first visit?
- within 2 weeks   1 1 1 1 1
- 2 weeks to 1 month   2 2 2 2 2
- 2 to 3 months   3 3 3 3 3
- 3 months or more   4 4 4 4 4
- DK   5 5 5 5 5
- NA   6 6 6 6 6

Have you taken her/him to a health centre or clinic since living in a hotel?
- yes   1 1 1 1 1
- no   2 2 2 2 2
- DK   3 3 3 3 3

IF YES: What did you go for last time?
[write]

IF NO: Do you know where the health centre or clinic is?
[write]

Has s/he had any vaccinations for:
- whooping cough?   1 1 1 1 1   ring
- diptheria/tetanus?   2 2 2 2 2   more
- polio?   3 3 3 3 3   than
- measles?   4 4 4 4 4   one
[NB. TRIPLE VACCINE = 1 AND 2]

REPEAT Q 5 - 16 FOR ALL CHILDREN UNDER 5

- 5 -

---

17. Since you moved into a hotel, has your child/children had to use the health services more, less or no different?
- more   1
- less   2
- no different 3
- DK   4
- NA   5

IF MORE OR LESS: Why is that?
[write]

18. Is there anything else you would like to say about your children's health since living in a hotel?
[write]

SECTION 4. CHILDREN'S PLAY

I want to ask you about your children's play. First of all, ... [NAME]

```
                                    Child aged:
                                    1) 1-2  2-3  3-4  4-5
```

19. How much time did s/he spend in the bedroom yesterday?
DAYTIME HOURS ONLY
PROBE IF SUNDAY
- under 2 hrs   2
- 5   5
- 8   8
- 8 or more
- DK

20. Is this typical?
[write]
- yes
- no, usual
- no, usual
- DK

21. Where does s/he play inside the hotel?
[write]
- bedroom
- common room
- halls/stairs
- other [write]
- DK

22. Are you happy with this or not? yes
[write]
- no, not safe
- no, complaints
- no, no space
- no, other
- DK

23. Does s/he go to any kind of playgroup or nursery at least once a week? no
[write which one]
- yes - playgrp
- yes - nursery
- yes - other
- DK

- 6 -

---

24. Before you moved into a hotel, did s/he go to any playgroup or nursery?
[write who and what]

IF USED TO GO BUT NOT NOW:
25. Why did s/he stop going?
[write]

REPEAT QUESTION 19 - 25 FOR ALL CHILDREN UNDER 5

Now can I ask about ... NAME ...

26. Has moving into a hotel affected your child/children?
- no   1
- not sure 2
- yes   3
- DK   4
- NA   5

IF YES: can you explain in what way?
[write]

27. Are there any play facilities you would like to have for your child/children?
[write]

SECTION 5. MOTHER'S HELP

I'd now like to ask about yourself.

28. Do you have any long-term health problems?
IF YES: Can yuou explain what this is?
[write]

- 7 -

---

29. Have you had any of the following illnesses since living in a hotel:
- chest infections?   1   ring
- diarrhoea?   2   more
- sickness/vomiting?   3   than
- bladder/kidney infections? 4   one
- burns or scald?   5
- severe headaches/migraine? 6
- anaemia?   7
- any other illnesses? [write] 8

30. Do you feel any of these:
- tired most of the time?   1   ring
- unhappy most of the time?   2   more
- children get on top of you?   3   than
- burst into tears for no reason?   4   one
- often lose your temper?   5
- often can't sleep at night?   6
- any other problems? [write]   7

31. Do you often take any medicines or pills (excluding contraceptive pills)?
- yes 1
- no   2
- DK   3

IF YES: What do you take?
[write]

32. Would you say your health is generally better, worse or about the same since moving into a hotel?
- better   1
- worse   2
- the same 3
- DK   4

IF BETTER OR WORSE: In what way?
[write]

33. If you are ill enough to need healp, where would you usually go?
[write]
- GP   1   ring
- clinic/health centre 2   more
- hospital   3   than
- other [write]   4   one
- DK   5

IF CLINIC/HEALTH CENTRE: Who do you see there?
[IF GP CODE 1]

- 8 -

34. Are you happy with this or not?
    - yes 1
    - no   2
    - DK   3

    IF NO: What are the problems?
    [write]

35. Are you registered with a GP?
    - no 1
    - yes - in this area temporarily 2
    - yes - in this area permanently 3
    - yes - in previous area 4
    - other [write] 5
    - DK 6

    PROBE: TEMPORARY OR PERMANENT
    THIS AND PREVIOUS AREA

36. Have you had any difficulties registering with a GP in this area?
    [write]
    - no 1
    - yes 2
    - not tried 3
    - DK 4

37. Have you had to go to a hospital since living in a hotel?
    - no 1
    - yes - inpatient 2   ring
    - yes - outpatient 3   more
    - yes - casualty 4   than
    - DK 5   one

    IF YES: How many times? What was this for?
    [write]

    IF CASUALTY: What time of day was this?
    [write]

38. Since you moved into a hotel, have you had to use the health services more, less or no different?
    [write]
    - more 1
    - less 2
    - no different 3
    - DK 4

    IF MORE OR LESS: Why is that?
    [write]

- 9 -

39. Since moving to a hotel, do you see more people to talk to, less or about the same?
    - more 1
    - less 2
    - the same 3
    - DK 4

    IF SEE MORE OR LESS: Why is that?
    [write]

40. How much time did you spend in the bedroom yesterday?
    DAYTIME HOURS ONLY
    PROBE IF SUNDAY
    - under 2 hours 1
    - 2 but under 5 hours 2
    - 5 but under 8 hours 3
    - 8 or more hours 4
    - DK 5

41. Is this typical?
    [write]
    - yes 1
    - no - more than usual 2
    - no - less than usual 3
    - DK 4

42. Is there anything else you would like to say about your general health since living in a hotel?
    [write]

SECTION 6. PREGNANCY

43. May I ask you if you have been pregnant while living in a hotel?
    - no S.8
    - yes - had abortion S.8
    - yes - had baby S.7
    - yes - stillborn/miscarriage
    - yes - pregnant now
    - DK

IF MISCARRIAGE OR STILLBORN:
44. At what stage was this?
    - under 12 weeks 1
    - 13 to 28 weeks 2
    - 28 weeks or more 3
    - DK 4
    - NA 5

    Do you know why this happened?
    [write]

    IF NO OTHER PREGNANCY: TO TO S.8

- 10 -

IF PREGNANT NOW:
45. How many weeks pregnant are you?
    - under 11 weeks 1
    - 12 to 17 weeks 2
    - 18 to 37 weeks 3
    - 38 weeks or more 4
    - DK 5

46. Have you booked into a hospital for the birth?
    - yes Y
    - no N
    - DK ?

    IF YES: Is the hospital nearby (within two miles)?
    - yes 1
    - no N
    - DK 5

    IF NO: Have you tried to transfer to a more local hospital?
    - yes 2
    - no 3
    - DK 4

    IF YES: What problems have you had?
    [write]

    IF NO: Why is that?
    [write]

47. Where are you going for antenatal care?
    - hospital [clinic] 1   ring
    - other clinic 2   more
    - GP 3   than
    - other [write] 4   one
    - nowhere 5
    - DK 6

    IF NOWHERE: Why is that?
    [write]

    IF CLINIC: Is the clinic nearby (within two miles)?
    - yes Y
    - no N
    - DK 5
    - NA 6

    IF NO: Have you tried to go to a more local clinic?
    - yes 2
    - no 3
    - DK 4

    IF YES: What problems have you had?

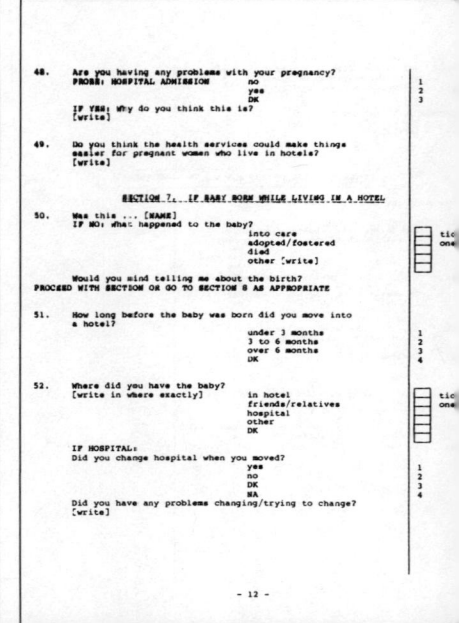

- 11 -

48. Are you having any problems with your pregnancy?
    PROBE: HOSPITAL ADMISSION
    - no 1
    - yes 2
    - DK 3

    IF YES: Why do you think this is?
    [write]

49. Do you think the health services could make things easier for pregnant women who live in hotels?
    [write]

SECTION 7. IF BABY BORN WHILE LIVING IN A HOTEL

50. Was this ... [NAME]
    IF NO: what happened to the baby?
    - into care
    - adopted/fostered
    - died
    - other [write]

    Would you mind telling me about the birth?
    PROCEED WITH SECTION OR GO TO SECTION 8 AS APPROPRIATE

51. How long before the baby was born did you move into a hotel?
    - under 3 months 1
    - 3 to 6 months 2
    - over 6 months 3
    - DK 4

52. Where did you have the baby?
    [write in where exactly]
    - in hotel
    - friends/relatives
    - hospital
    - other
    - DK

    IF HOSPITAL:
    Did you change hospital when you moved?
    - yes 1
    - no 2
    - DK 3
    - NA 4

    Did you have any problems changing/trying to change?
    [write]

- 12 -

Questionnaire for women in bed and breakfast

53. Where did you go for antenatal care?

hospital	1
clinic	2
GP	3
other [write]	4
nowhere	5
DK	6

ring more than one

IF NOWHERE: Why was that?
[write]

IF CLINIC:
Did you try to change clinic when you moved?
IF YES: Did you have any problems?
[write]

54. Did you have any problems with your pregnancy?
PROBE FOR HOSPITAL ADMISSION

yes	1
no	2
DK	3

IF YES: Why do you think you had problems?
[write]

55. Was your pregnancy full term?

yes	1
no	2
DK	3

IF NO: How early was the baby born?
[write]

56. How much did the baby weigh at birth?

under 3lb 4oz (1,500 kg)	1
3lb 5oz to 5lb 5oz	2
over 5lb 5oz (s,500 kg)	3
DK	4

57. Was the baby healthy at birth?

yes	1
no	2
DK	3

IF NO: What was the problem?
[write] PROBE: NEED FOR SPECIAL CARE/HANDICAPPED

- 13 -

---

58. How long did you stay in hospital altogether?

up to 2 days	1
3 to 4 days	2
5 to 9 days	3
10 to 15 days	4
16 or more days	5
DK	6

59. Did the baby stay in longer?
[write]

PROCEED TO QUESTION 61

SECTION 8. MOVING TO HOTEL WITH NEW BABY

60. Did you move into a hotel straight after your [youngest] child was born?

yes	1
no	2
DK	3
NA	4

tick one

IF NO, DK OR NA, GO TO SECTION 9

61. How old was the baby when you came back to/moved into the hotel?

straight from hospital	1
not, but within 2 weeks	2
not, but 2 to 4 weeks	3
not, but 5 to 8 weeks	4
not, but over 8 weeks	5
DK	6

- 14 -

---

62. Where there any particular problems bringing a new baby back to a hotel?
[write]

no	1
yes - all in one room	2
yes - room too small	3
yes - noise from others	4
yes - baby's noise	5
yes - feeding	6
yes - keeping warm	7
yes - nappies	8
yes - dirty	9
yes - other [write]	10
DK	11

ring more than one

IF MORE THAN ONE CHILD:
63. Who looked after your other child/children when you first came to the hotel with the baby?
[write]

64. Did you have a postnatal check after six weeks?

yes	1
no	2
DK	3

IF NO: Why was this?
[write]

65. Have you had any problems since the birth?

yes	1
no	2
DK	3

IF YES: Do you think this was affected by living in hotel?
[write]

66. Do you think the health services could make things easier for women in hotels when they have a baby?
[write]

- 15 -

SECTION 9. FOOD AND EATING

Now I want to ask about what you eat.

67. Can you tell me what you ate yesterday?
[ASK TYPE OF BREAD AND MILK]

Item/how cooked   Quantity

Did you have anything before breakfast?

Did you have breakfast?

And after breakfast

What about lunch?

Any snacks in the afternoon?

And tea?

Anything later on?

And before going to bed?

- 16 -

130 PRESCRIPTION FOR POOR HEALTH

68. Was yesterday a typical day?
    IF NO: In what way?
    [write]

69. Do you eat different things at the weekend?
    [write]

70. How many times a week do you eat any of the following?

    (Tick a box)
    Days a week

Milk in pints	7	4-6	1-3	1	never
Bread					
Chappatis					
Fresh fruit					
Fruit juice in cartons					
Fresh/frozen vegetables					
Salad vegetables					
Baked beans					
Dahl/dried peas/beans					
Tinned spaghetti					
Rice/pasta					
Potatoes/yams/plantain					
Pasties/pies/sausages/burgers etc					
Tinned meat eg. corned beef					
Fresh/frozen meat					

    - 17 -

Days a week

	7	4-6	1-3	1	never
Fish and chips					
Fish fingers					
Tinned fish (eg. sardines, pilchards)					
Dried salt fish					
Other fresh or frozen fish					
Cheese					
Yoghurt					
Eggs					
Dried packet meals eg. pot noodle					
Dried packet soups					
Frozen meals					
Cakes and biscuits					
Sweets and chocolates					
Packet or frozen desserts					

- 18 -

71. Altogether, roughly how many times a week do you:
    eat hotel meals?   No. ....   office
    eat in cafes?   No. ....   code
    eat take-aways?   No. ....
    prepare own meals?   No. ....
    other? [write]   No. ....

72. Are there any differences between what you eat and what your child/children eat?
    IF YES: In what way?
    [write]

73. Do you have any cooking facilities or kettle in your room?
    yes   Y
    no   1
    DK   8

    IF YES: What do you have?
    kettle   2   ring
    rings   3   more
    grill   4   than
    oven   5   one
    microwave   6
    other [write]   7

    Is this satisfactory?
    PROBE FOR SAFETY
    [write]

74. Is there a kitchen you can use?
    yes   Y
    no   1
    DK   9

    IF YES: Where is it in relation to your room?
    attached to room   2
    same floor   3
    one floor away   4
    two or more floors away 5
    other [write]   6
    DK   7
    NA   8

    What cooking facilities are there and how many work?
    rings   ... No
    grill   ... No
    oven   ... No
    other [write] ... No

- 19 -

How many other families share it (apart from your family)?   ... No
Do you use it?
    yes   1
    no   2
    DK   3
    NA   4

Is the kitchen satisfactory?
[write]
    yes   1   ring
    no - too far away   2   more
    no - dirty   3   than
    no - too many use it   4   one
    no - restrictions [write]   5
    no - other [write]   6
                                   7
    DK   8
    NA

75. Where do you keep your food?
    [write]
    fridge in kitchen   1   ring
    fridge in bedroom   2   more
    fridge elsewhere [write]   3   than
    cupboard in kitchen   4   one
    cupboard in bedroom   5
    windowsill   6
    elsewhere in bedroom   7
    other [write]   8
    don't keep any food   9
    DK   10

76. Is this satisfactory?
    PROBE: any other problems?
    yes   1   ring
    no - fridge   2   more
    no - fridge/cupboard too small   3   than
    no - fridge/cupboard dirty   4   one
    no - food gets stolen   5
    no - food goes off   6
    no - cockroaches, bugs etc   7
    no - other [write]   8
    DK   9
    NA   10

77. What about preparing food: is this alright or are there problems?
    yes - alright   1
    no - problems   N
    DK   7

    IF NO: What are the problems?
    [write]
    nowhere suitable   2   ring
    too dirty   3   more
    too far from room   4   than
    dangerous   5   one
    other [write]   6

- 20 -

Questionnaire for women in bed and breakfast

IF CHILD UNDER 2 YEARS:
78. Is it easy or difficult for you to prepare the baby's bottles and baby food?
    - easy — 1
    - difficult — 2
    - DK — 6
    - NA — 7

    IF DIFFICULT: In what way?
    [write]
    - difficult - warming — 2 ring
    - difficult - cleaning — 3 more
    - difficult - storage — 4 than
    - other [write] — 5 one

79. Thinking about your children (under 5) in particular, can you give them the kind of food you want to?
    - yes — 1
    - no — 2
    - DK — 3
    - NA — 4

    IF NO: Why is this?
    [write]

80. Roughly how much a week do you usually spend on food for your whole family?
    - under £10 — 1
    - £11 - 20 — 2
    - £21 - 30 — 3
    - £31 - 40 — 4
    - £41 - 50 — 5
    - £51 or more — 6
    - DK — 7

81. Looking at food and eating overall are you happy or do you have problems?
    - happy — 1
    - have problems — 9
    - DK — 9

    IF PROBLEMS: What are the problems?
    [write]
    - expensive — 2 ring
    - dieting limited/boring — 3 more
    - bad diet — 4 than
    - can't eat food of choice — 5 one
    - often feel hungry — 6
    - nowhere to sit and eat — 7
    - other [write] — 8

- 21 -

82. Compared with the time before you lived in a hotel, do you now eat better, as well or less well?
    - better — 1
    - as well — 2
    - less well — 3
    - DK — 4

    IF BETTER OR LESS WELL: In what way?
    [write]

SECTION 10. ACCOMMODATION

How can you tell me about your room and the hotel. First of all:
83. How many bedrooms do you and your family have to yourselves? ... No.

    IF MORE THAN ONE:
    How far apart are your rooms?
    [write]
    - adjacent — 1
    - same floor — 2
    - one floor apart — 3
    - one floor apart — 4
    - other [write] — 5
    - DK — 6
    - NA — 7

84. Roughly how big is the main bedroom?
    ... feet long X ... feet wide
    IF OTHER BEDROOM(S): How big is the other room(s)?
    ... feet long X ... feet wide   ... sq ft together

85. Does your child/children have to share their bed(s) with anyone else?
    [write]
    - no — 1
    - yes, with another child — 2
    - yes, with an adult — 3
    - DK — 4
    - NA — 5

86. What floor level is the main bedroom on? (Ground = 0) ... No.
    IF THIRD OR ABOVE: Is there a lift?
    - yes — Y
    - no — 1
    - DK — 5
    - NA — 6

    IF YES: Is it reliable?
    [write]
    - yes — 2
    - no — 3
    - DK — 4

- 22 -

87. Is the heating in your room satisfactory or not?
    - yes — 1
    - no — N
    - DK — 9

    IF NO: Why is that?
    PROBE FOR DRAUGHTS
    [write]
    - no heating — 2 ring
    - too hot — 3 more
    - too cold — 4 than
    - can't control — 5 one
    - stuffy/can't ventilate — 6
    - draughty — 7
    - other [write] — 8

88. Is your room damp or mouldy?
    - yes — Y
    - no — 1
    - DK — 6

    IF YES: In what way?
    [write]
    - generally damp — 2 ring
    - damp patches — 3 more
    - mould — 4 than
    - other [write] — 5 one

89. Where is the nearest working toilet?
    - adjacent to room — 1
    - same floor — 2
    - 1 floor away — 3
    - 2 or more floors away — 4
    - other [write] — 5

90. How many other people share the toilet (apart from your family)? ... No.

91. Where is the nearest bath or shower which works?
    - in room — 1
    - adjacent to room — 2
    - same floor — 3
    - 1 floor away — 4
    - 2 or more floors away — 5
    - other [write] — 6
    - DK — 7

92. How many other people share it (apart from your family)? ... No.

93. Does the bath or shower have hot water?
    PROBE: Can you use it all the time?
    [write]
    - yes - always — 1
    - yes - sometimes [write] — 2
    - no - never — 3
    - DK — 4

- 23 -

94. Where is the nearest washbasin or sink which works?
    [write]
    - in room — 1
    - adjacent to room — 2
    - same floor — 3
    - 1 floor away — 4
    - 2 or more floors away — 5
    - other [write] — 6
    - DK — 7

95. How many other people share it (apart from your family)? ... No.

96. Does the washbasin or sink have hot water?
    PROBE: Can you use it all the time?
    [write]
    - yes - always — 1
    - yes - sometimes [write] — 2
    - no - never — 3
    - DK — 4

Thinking now about washing and drying clothes:
98. Where do you usually wash clothes?
    - bedroom — 1 ring
    - kitchen — 2 more
    - bathroom — 3 than
    - hotel laundry — 4 one
    - public laundrette — 5
    - friends/relatives — 6
    - other [write] — 7
    - DK — 8

97. Where do you usually wash clothes?
    - bedroom — 1 ring
    - kitchen — 2 more
    - bathroom — 3 than
    - hotel laundry — 4 one
    - public laundrette — 5
    - friends/relatives — 6
    - other [write] — 7
    - use disposables — 8
    - NA — 9

99. Where do you usually dry clothes?
    [write]
    - bedroom — 1 ring
    - balcony — 2 more
    - bathroom — 3 than
    - hotel laundry — 4 one
    - public laundrette — 5
    - friends/relatives — 6
    - other [write] — 7
    - DK — 8

- 24 -

132 PRESCRIPTION FOR POOR HEALTH

100. Is washing or drying clothes a problem here or not?
    - yes — Y
    - no — 1
    - DK — 6

    IF YES: In what way?
    - expensive — 2   ring
    - makes room damp — 3   more
    - no space to dry — 4   than
    - other [write] — 5   one

101. Do you use the hotel sheets?
    - yes — Y 1
    - no — 7
    - DK

    IF YES: How often do you get clean ones?
    - at least weekly — 2
    - at least fortnightly — 3
    - at least monthly — 4
    - other [write] — 5
    - DK — 6

102. Does the hotel clean your room (hoovering)?
    - yes — Y 1
    - no — 8
    - DK

    IF YES: How often?
    - daily — 2
    - at least weekly — 3
    - at least fortnightly — 4
    - at least monthly — 5
    - other [write] — 6
    - DK — 7

103. Generally, is the hotel clean or not?
    - yes — Y 1
    - no — N 7
    - DK

    IF NO: In what way?
    - WC/bathroom dirty — 2   ring
    - kitchen dirty — 3   more
    - bedroom dirty — 4   than
    - fleas/bugs/cockroaches — 5   one
    - other [write] — 6

104. Is getting rid of rubbish a problem or not?
    - yes — 1
    - no — 2
    - DK — 3

    IF YES: In what way?
    [write] PROBE FOR HAPPIES

- 25 -

105. Do you think the hotel is a safe place or not?
    - yes — 1
    - no — 2
    - DK — 3

    IF NO: In what way?
    PROBE FOR LIGHTING IN HALLS AND STAIRS
    [write]

    INTERVIEWER'S OBSERVATIONS: WIRING/GAS AND ELECTRIC
    FITTINGS/FLOORS/STAIRS/FIRE RISKS.

106. Do the fire alarms work?
    [write]
    - yes — seem to — 1
    - no — aren't any — 2
    - never heard them — 3
    - ring too often — 4
    - other [write] — 5
    - Dk — 6

107. Where is the nearest working phone you can use?
    PROBE FOR RESTRICTIONS
    - own room — 1
    - same floor — 2
    - 1 floor away — 3
    - 2 or more floors away — 4
    - outside hotel, nearby — 5
    - outside hotel, distant — 6
    - DK — 7

108. What do you think generally about your room and this hotel?
    [write] PROBE: PRIVACY/SECURITY/TENSIONS/NOISE

SECTION 11. HOUSING STATUS

Can I now ask:
109. How long have you lived in this hotel?
    - under 3 months — 1
    - 3 to 5 months — 2
    - 6 to 11 months — 3
    - 12 to 24 months — 4
    - over 2 years — 5
    - DK — 6

- 26 -

110. Altogether, how much time have you spent living in hotels during the last five years?
    - under 3 months — 1
    - 3 to 5 months — 2
    - 6 to 11 months — 3
    - 1-2 years — 4
    - 2-3 years — 5
    - 3-4 years — 6
    - 4-5 years — 7
    - 5 or more years — 8
    - DK — 9

111. How many times have you moved in the last year?
    (include moves within a hotel)
    [write] ... No.

112. Were you placed in this hotel by a council?
    - yes — 1
    - no — 2
    - DK — 3

    IF YES:
    Which council is that?   name ....
    When did you last have any contact with the housing department? (Go right back to last contact.) ... weeks

113. IF PLACED BY COUNCILS: How far from .... are you now in terms of the time it takes to travel there?
    IF NOT PLACED BY COUNCIL: How far away was your last home in terms of the time it takes to travel there?
    - under 15 minutes — 1
    - 15 to 29 minutes — 2
    - 30 to 59 minutes — 3
    - 1 to 2 hours — 4
    - over 2 hours — 5
    - DK — 6

ASK ALL:
114. Have you any idea how long you might stay here?
    [write]
    - no idea — 1
    - under 1 month — 2
    - 1 to 5 months — 3
    - 6 to 11 months — 4
    - 12 months or more — 5
    - for ever — 6

- 27 -

SECTION 12. EMPLOYMENT AND INCOME

Now I want to ask a few questions about work and money.

	F	M
115. Are you (or your partner) working now?
    - yes, full time — 1 1   ring
    - yes, part time — 2 2   one
    - no, unemployed, seeking work — 3 3
    - no, unemployed, not seeking work — 4 4
    - no, sick — 5 5
    - no, student — 6 6
    - other [write] — 7 7
    - DK — 8 8

IF YES:
116. Does living here affect your work (your partner's work) in any way?
    - yes — Y Y
    - no — 1 1
    - DK — 6 6
    - NA — 7 7

    IF YES: In what way?
    - wage too low for hotel — 2 2   ring
    - journey to work — 3 3   more
    - tired/stressed — 4 4   than
    - other [write] — 5 5   one

IF NO:
117. Did you (or your partner) have a job just before moving here?
    - yes — Y Y
    - no — 1 1
    - DK — 6 6
    - NA — 7 7

    IF YES: Why did you (your partner) stop working?
    [write]
    - couldn't afford hotel — 2 2   ring
    - journey to work — 3 3   more
    - tired/stressed — 4 4   than
    - other [write] — 5 5   one

IF NO, UNEMPLOYED:
118. Does living here affect your search for work/ whether yuou look for work?
    - yes — Y Y
    - no — 1 1
    - DK — 8 8
    - NA — 9 9

    IF YES: In what way?
    [write]
    - wages too low for hotel — 2 2   ring
    - journey to work — 3 3   more
    - hotel residents refused — 4 4   than
    - don't know where will live — 5 5   one
    - other [write] — 6 6
    - DK — 7 7

- 28 -

ASK ALL:
119. What is your total household income in an average week, including any benefits? [net income]
    IF WORKING: Does that include FIS, HB, Child Ben, Sup Ben, Mat Ben etc?
    IF NOT WORKING: Does that include Unemp Ben, Sup Ben, Sick Ben, Child Ben, Mat Ben, etc?
    £ ... net

120. Do you pay for this room?
    not at all
    yes - to landlord   tick
    yes - to council
    yes - other [write]
    DK
    IF YES: How much do you pay each week?   £ ... cost

121. Do you have to pay for anything else. For example: heating: what does this cost a week?   £ ... cost
    hot water/baths: what does this cost a week?   £ ... cost
    kitchen/cooking: what does this cost a week?   £ ... cost
    electricity: what does this cost a week?   £ ... cost
    TV: what does this cost a week?   £ ... cost
    anything else? [write]   £ ... cost   £ ... total cost

122. Do you or your children have to go without anything because you can't afford it?
    yes   Y
    no   1
    DK   11
    IF YES: what do you go without?
    [write]
        own food   2   ring
        children's food   3   more
        own clothes/shoes   4   than
        children's clothes/shoes 5 one
        heat   6
        trips out   7
        holidays   8
        toys/equipment   9
        other [write]   10

- 29 -

123. How would you describe your ethnic origin?
    SHOW CARD   ....
    IF PARTNER: What ethnic origin is your partner/husband?   ....

Finally:

SECTION 13. FINALLY

124. Apart from the things you have mentioned already, are there any other ways in which living in a hotel has affected you or your children?
    [write]

125. What are your general feelings about living here?
    [write]

126. Do you think the council housing department could do anything to help families with children living in hotels?
    [write]

127. Do you think the health service could do anything to help families with children living in hotels?
    [write]

Thank you very much for your help.
We're talking to lots of other women in hotels and will then write a report. We hope that be showing what it's like to live in a hotel, something will be done to make things better.

- 30 -

Appendix 2
Data collection sheet for health records

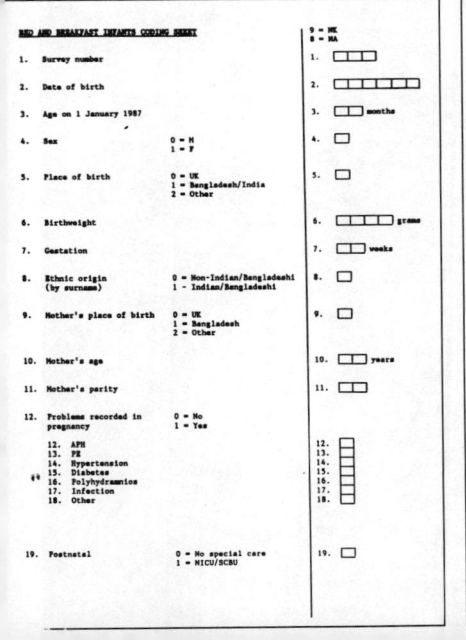

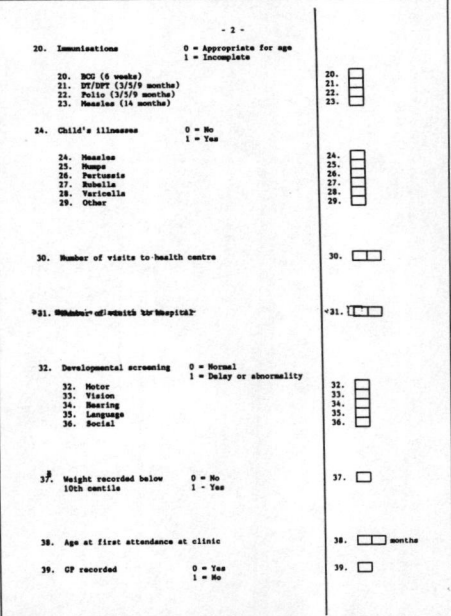

BED AND BREAKFAST INFANTS CODING SHEET 9 = NK
 8 = NA

1. Survey number 1. ☐☐☐

2. Date of birth 2. ☐☐☐☐☐☐

3. Age on 1 January 1987 3. ☐☐ months

4. Sex 0 = M 4. ☐
   1 = F

5. Place of birth 0 = UK 5. ☐
   1 = Bangladesh/India
   2 = Other

6. Birthweight 6. ☐☐☐☐ grams

7. Gestation 7. ☐☐ weeks

8. Ethnic origin 0 = Non-Indian/Bangladeshi 8. ☐
   (by surname) 1 = Indian/Bangladeshi

9. Mother's place of birth 0 = UK 9. ☐
   1 = Bangladesh
   2 = Other

10. Mother's age 10. ☐☐ years

11. Mother's parity 11. ☐☐

12. Problems recorded in 0 = No
    pregnancy 1 = Yes
    12. APH 12. ☐
    13. PE 13. ☐
    14. Hypertension 14. ☐
    15. Diabetes 15. ☐
    16. Polyhydramnios 16. ☐
    17. Infection 17. ☐
    18. Other 18. ☐

19. Postnatal 0 = No special care 19. ☐
    1 = NICU/SCBU

- 2 -

20. Immunisations 0 = Appropriate for age
    1 = Incomplete
    20. BCG (6 weeks) 20. ☐
    21. DT/DPT (3/5/9 months) 21. ☐
    22. Polio (3/5/9 months) 22. ☐
    23. Measles (14 months) 23. ☐

24. Child's illnesses 0 = No
    1 = Yes
    24. Measles 24. ☐
    25. Mumps 25. ☐
    26. Pertussis 26. ☐
    27. Rubella 27. ☐
    28. Varicella 28. ☐
    29. Other 29. ☐

30. Number of visits to health centre 30. ☐☐

31. Number of visits to hospital 31. ☐☐☐

32. Developmental screening 0 = Normal
    1 = Delay or abnormality
    32. Motor 32. ☐
    33. Vision 33. ☐
    34. Hearing 34. ☐
    35. Language 35. ☐
    36. Social 36. ☐

37. Weight recorded below 0 = No 37. ☐
    10th centile 1 = Yes

38. Age at first attendance at clinic 38. ☐☐☐ months

39. GP recorded 0 = Yes 39. ☐
    1 = No

Appendix 2
Data collection sheet for health records